Cover photo by San Diego Zoo.
Frontispiece by Glen S. Axelrod.

Front endpapers: Umbrella cockatoo. Photo courtesy of San Diego Zoo.
Back endpapers: Yellow-tailed black cockatoo. Photo courtesy of San Diego Zoo.

ISBN 0-87666-826-0

Distributed in the U.S. by T.F.H. Publications, Inc., 211 West Sylvania Avenue, PO Box 427, Neptune, NJ 07753; in England by T.F.H. (Gt. Britain) Ltd., 13 Nutley Lane, Reigate, Surrey; in Canada to the pet trade by Rolf C. Hagen Ltd., 3225 Sartelon Street, Montreal 382, Quebec; in Canada to the book trade by H & L Pet Supplies, Inc., 27 Kingston Crescent, Kitchener, Ontario; in Southeast Asia by Y.W. Ong, 9 Lorong 36 Geylang, Singapore 14; in Australia and the South Pacific by Pet Imports Pty. Ltd., P.O. Box 149, Brookvale 2100, N.S.W. Australia; in South Africa by Valid Agencies, P.O. Box 51901, Randburg 2125 South Africa. Published by T.F.H. Publications, Inc., Ltd, the British Crown Colony of Hong Kong.

HANDBOOK OF COCKATOOS

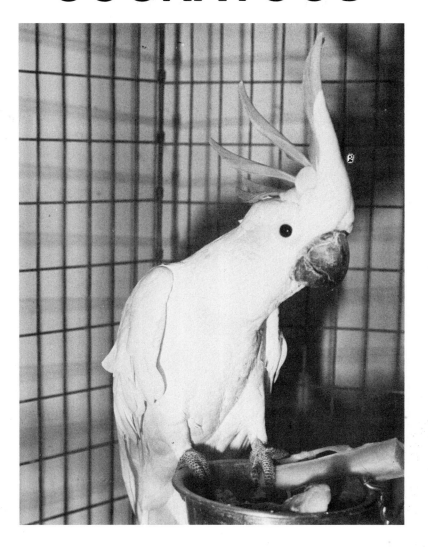

DR. A.E. DECOTEAU

Above: The many different cockatoo species range in size from Goffin's cockatoo, which averages 12″ in length, to much larger cockatoos such as the Moluccan, which averages about 24″ in length. Photo by Glen S. Axelrod. **Opposite:** Aside from great differences in size, cockatoo species exhibit a variety of colors, from pure white to charcoal-gray or black. This is a black palm cockatoo. Photo by Steve Kates.

Contents

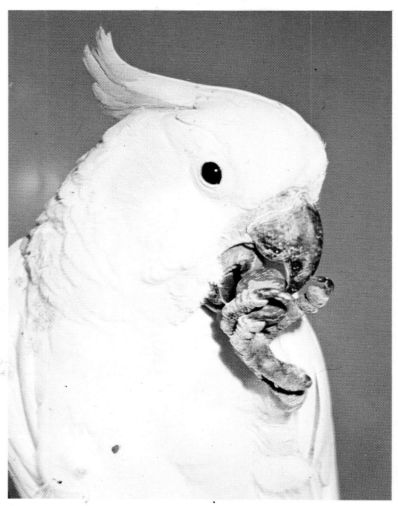

Because Australia has banned the export of birds, many cockatoo species are not readily available in the United States. The lesser sulphur-crested cockatoo, however, is native to the Celebes and Indonesia and, as it is commonly imported, is usually available in this country. Photo by A.J. Mobbs.

Opposite:
The gang-gang cockatoo is native to Australia and is rarely seen in the United States. Photo courtesy of San Diego Zoo.

Acknowledgments

I am indebted to Cliff Bickford of the Miami area for his excellent contribution of good quality colored photos. His interest in photography and birds is most gratifying.

The continued interest and participation by my family is most worthwhile to me; Helen my wife and my sons Daren, Jay and Kevin share my interests in parrots. Daren is particularly involved, not only as one of the finest young bird judges today, but also as a young man with a keen interest in working and training cockatoos.

This book is dedicated to
DAREN DECOTEAU

Preface

We have entered an era in which parrots, and particularly cockatoos, have entered the homes of thousands of pet owners and countless more breeders and aviculturists. Because the time for importations of these birds will soon come to an end, the need to breed the cockatoos is quite evident. With the constant destruction of forests and other natural habitats of the birds on various Pacific islands as well as in Indonesia and other larger land masses, there will be no more rare birds in the next century. It is indeed time to breed these birds, to learn their habits, to discover their likes and dislikes in foodstuffs and to treasure their existence so future generations can see them.

When I was quite young, I walked into a better than ordinary pet shop; there I saw for the first time the most beautiful creature I had ever seen. It was called a greater sulphur-crested cockatoo. As I walked into the back room, I was more impressed with another bird which was even more lustrous, the salmon-crested cockatoo! Let us hope our future generations have this chance to see firsthand such beauty.

Numerous books have been written, many in the past four years, on parrots including cockatoos. Every author and every breeder has his or her way to feed, breed, care for, exhibit and train cockatoos. This book attempts to give some methods in accomplishing these things. I also describe many factual events and situations which might give you a few minutes of enjoyment and, even more important, give you an idea of how to better handle and care for your bird.

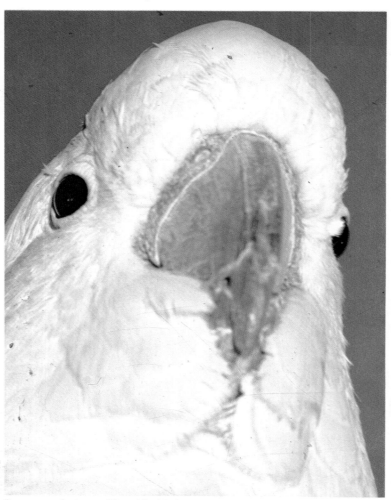

Some cockatoos, like this Moluccan, have the ability to bring their cheek feathers over the mandible. Photo by Cliff Bickford.

Opposite:
Cockatoos are probably best known for their backward or forward curving crests. The crest of an Eleonora cockatoo (upper photo) curves forward, while the crests of Moluccans (lower photo) curve backward. Upper photo by Dr. A.E. Decoteau; lower photo by Glen S. Axelrod.

These Leadbeater or Major Mitchell's cockatoos exemplify all of the characteristics which make cockatoos such excellent pets and show birds—they have pleasing personalities, exhibit noble behavior, display extraordinary beauty and breed in captivity. Photo courtesy of San Diego Zoo.

GENERAL INFORMATION

The Cockatoo In General

Perhaps one of the most unusual and attractive of the great parrot family is the cockatoo. In each and every case, the cockatoo is best known for its crest. Some of the crests are small; some are large. Certain crests curve forward; others curve backward. There are some crests that are noticeable when at rest; others appear as if they don't exist when at rest.

Some crests are bright red, some are brilliant yellow, one is orange-yellow and several are either white, black, rose or pink. One beautiful crest is red, yellow and white.

Cockatoos are able to erect their crests at will. Most often they display their crests when irritated, nervous, excited or happy. They most certainly display their crest as a court-ship display to their mates.

All cockatoos are placed in one of three main categories: they are either mostly white in general body color, a variety of black or pink. Further, the pink cockatoos fall into the general white grouping since the main color is white tinged with pastel pink or rose. One could then classify cockatoos as mostly white or mostly black with one intermediate. The white cockatoos are:

Umbrella, all white, crest included.
Cacatua alba
Sulphur-crested group, all white, yellow crest, greater in size.
Cacatua galerita galerita

Most cockatoos have dark-colored beaks and claws, both of which might need occasional trimming. The strong black beak of this blue-eyed cockatoo is partially hidden by the cheek feathers. Photo by Cliff Bickford.

Opposite:
When they are eating, cockatoos usually use one of their feet like a hand to hold food. This Moluccan (upper photo) looks like it's tasting the fruit to determine if it likes the fruit's flavor. The greater sulphur-crested cockatoo (lower photo) is displaying a typical cockatoo pastime—preening. Upper photo by Kerry V. Donnelly; lower photo by Dr. Herbert R. Axelrod.

Cacatua galerita fitzroyi
Cacatua galerita triton
Cacatua galerita eleonora
Sulphur-crested group, all white, yellow crest, smaller in size.
Cacatua sulphurea sulphurea
Cacatua sulphurea djampeana
Cacatua sulphurea abbotti
Cacatua sulphurea occidentalis
Cacatua sulphurea parvula
Cacatua sulphurea citrinocristata (this one has an orange-yellow crest)
Blue-eyed, white body, yellow crest.
Cacatua ophthalmica
Smaller whites, small white crests, other identifying features.
Cacatua haematuropygia
Cacatua goffini
Cacatua sanguinea sanguinea
Cacatua sanguinea normantoni
Cacatua tenuirostris tenuirostris
Cacatua tenuirostris pastinator
Cacatua ducorps
White body plumage, pastel pink throughout, darker red crests.
Cacatua leadbeateri leadbeateri
Cacatua leadbeateri mollis
Cacatua moluccensis

The black cockatoos are characterized by varying shades of black, from a distinct black to a light charcoal color and to a light gray. Some feathers are even edged in pinkish or red tones.

Charcoal black, bare red face.
Probosciger aterrimus aterrimus
Probosciger aterrimus goliath
Probosciger aterrimus stenolophus

Rose-breasted cockatoos are treasured in the United States, but in their native Australia these birds are slaughtered as pests. Photo by John Warham.

Black with varying tail colors.
Calyptorhynchus funereus funereus
Calyptorhynchus funereus baudinii
Calyptorhynchus magnificus
Calyptorhynchus lathami
Gray with red head on male, red breast shadings on female.
Callocephalon fimbriatum

Finally, we get to the intermediate which is gray about the back, wings and tail, but with a distinct pink or rose color on the entire breast. This species could very well be the connecting link between the two other major color groups of cockatoos.
Eolophus roseicapillus

21

Above: Cockatoos are incessant chewers and will eventually destroy anything made of wood in their cages. The wooden supports of this aviary for Moluccan cockatoos are covered by wire mesh. Photo by Earl Grossman. **Opposite:** The rose-breasted cockatoo perched on top of the cage is allowed the freedom of the room, while the sulphur-crested cockatoo is restricted to its cage because of the damage it does to the room with its beak when allowed freedom. The cage has heavy padlocks on the door and a steel perch because "Plato" can bite through ordinary locks and can even demolish a mahogany perch in a day. The bird is, however, an excellent talker and a very loveable and superb-looking pet. Photo by Ray Hanson.

It is also noteworthy to mention that the cockatoo is, in general, quite easy to sex. Since most species and subspecies of cockatoos have distinguishable sexes, it is much easier to match pairs, thereby alleviating the need for long-standing experience for the potential breeder of this splendid category of parrot. All of the white cockatoos except one can be sexed by closely examining the color of the eye. If the eye is brownish red in color, then it is a female. A solid black eye is typical of the male. It has been said by "overnight experts" that this is not factual. I do not agree with these "experts" because I have mated many pairs with excellent results. Some so-called "experts" have stated that with the advent of the endoscope and the laparascope, they have determined that sex is not always correlated with eye color; but I have endoscoped numerous males and females with the result that the eye color has proved the sex of the bird one hundred percent of the time.

It is important to indicate that the slender-billed cockatoo (or long-billed corella) cannot be sexed by eye color. Another species that is most difficult to sex by eye color is the Moluccan or salmon-crested cockatoo. However, if one shines a light directly into the eye, he can differentiate the sex quite readily.

With few exceptions, black cockatoos are even easier to sex. The red-tailed, glossy and gang-gang cockatoos can easily be differentiated by distinct differences in color. The other blacks are tougher to differentiate except for quite obvious differences in size between the sexes. This is particularly noticeable with the great black palm cockatoo; this, however, is sometimes also deceiving.

All cockatoos originate geographically in the South Pacific, with many of them being native to Australia. Some cockatoos, such as the black palm, are found extensively in New Guinea and in northern Australia. Others, such as Goffin's cockatoo, are found only on a few islands, such as the now de-forested Tanimbar Islands off the Indonesian

There are indications that a few cockatoos might soon face extinction; domestic breeding of cockatoos, though, will preserve them for future generations. This has been done, for example, with birds such as the turquoisine parakeets shown above. Photo by Harry V. Lacey.

Cockatoos love to be stroked as well as spoken to. They can learn to imitate human speech, but they are not the best talkers of the bird world. Photo by Ray Hanson.

Opposite:
Hand-fed cockatoos (upper photo) are usually easier to tame and train because they are used to your company and have learned to trust and depend on you. Even the friendliest cockatoo, however, will give an occasional nip (lower photo). With a tame bird it is only a friendly nip, and this owner has learned from experience that the bird will not hurt her. Upper photo by Manolo Guevara; lower photo by Ray Hanson.

coast. These islands have been denuded of their forests, thereby placing the Goffin's cockatoo in grave danger of becoming extinct.

There are many parrots included on either the endangered species list or the threatened list; however, there are no cockatoos currently listed as endangered. My prediction is that within the present decade one will see the fading of at least two species or subspecies of cockatoo. It is entirely too sad that too many people believe that the exporters and importers of parrots and, in this case, cockatoos are doing harm to the various species of birds. Indeed this is not true since there are numerous species I can name that have been saved by the exporter and/or importer and, in turn, the breeder. By domestically breeding certain rare species, dedicated aviculturists have saved them for future generations to enjoy. The Nene goose, the scarlet-chested parakeet and the turquoisine parakeet are excellent examples. The Bali mynah is another species saved by the excellence of aviculture. In other instances, the cause of extinction and apparent reduction of species and subspecies too often rests with man. The jungle habitat of many species is being ravaged, burned, deforested for lumber, cleared for settlements and agriculture or flooded for irrigation. Because of this danger, aviculturists must be allowed to take these birds and breed them for the benefit of the species and mankind.

As a talker, the cockatoo does not compare to the African grey or various Amazons. It is in itself a good talker since I have seen several cockatoos that had fairly good vocabularies. In general, however, most cockatoos say few words.

As a pet, the cockatoo cannot be excelled. My son Daren has tamed a cockatoo within two hours on more than one occasion. The birds become very docile as well as extremely loyal. Daren can place his fingers between the mandibles of several different cockatoos with no danger of getting bitten.

They tend to give him a mild squeeze as if to say, "You are my friend."

When one does have a cockatoo as a pet, he must not be disturbed by the production of powder from the feathers of the birds. This powder is normal and will collect like dust, particularly in white cockatoos.

Cockatoos are rather poor eaters, particularly when new to a home. Often they will absolutely not eat in front of a human and would rather wait until they are alone. Unlike other parrots, they do not like all types of foods. I have found that they eat much less than a macaw, an Amazon or even an African grey. In fact, I have had some cockatoos that frightened me because they ate much less than lovebirds I have owned. When acclimated, however, they will begin to eat much more readily. They will also start to eat fruit when it is offered.

As breeders, cockatoos are much easier to work with than Amazons, macaws and other larger parrots. I have found that once they are mature, cockatoos become excellent breeding birds, giving one much success. Both sexes participate in the incubation and the feeding of the babies, whereas very few other parrot species have the male as a participant in brooding.

Sadly, though, in many species of cockatoos unless you remove the babies and hand-feed them, one of the babies will be allowed to die by the parents.

The cockatoo is extremely popular as a pet and as a breeding bird. It is also an exhibition bird at many bird shows due to its aristocratic behavior, its calmness and its breathtaking splendor.

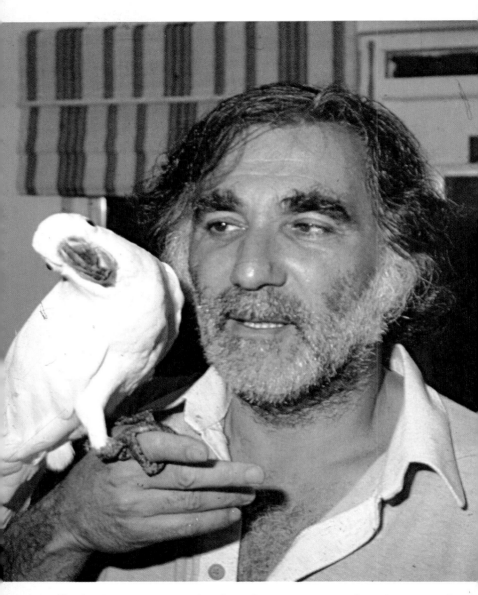

Cockatoos are so popular that pirates are smuggling them out of their native ranges and bringing them into North America and Europe, where importation of parrot-like birds is strictly regulated.

Cockatoos are notorious wood-chewers. This cockatoo has already done some damage to a large wooden perch and continues to enjoy chewing on a tasty morsel from it. Photo by Kerry Donnelly.

Housing Your Cockatoo

One must be innovative when considering the proper housing for the cockatoo. There is no parrot-type bird that chews wood as much as the cockatoo. One must therefore be very cautious before building an aviary made entirely or partially of wood. When building a large aviary, it is best to use hardware cloth with a one-half-inch mesh. Any wood braces must be wired over so the cockatoos cannot get to it to chew it up.

In order to house two large breeding birds that will be happy and content, the dimensions for a cockatoo aviary must be carefully thought out. I prefer an aviary that is three feet wide, eight feet high and twelve feet long. I always place two nest boxes or nest logs in a pen such as this so the breeding pair can select the site they prefer. Place plenty of thick perches within the aviary.

If you are going to breed your birds, you should have an aviary that will be conducive to their breeding. I have also utilized a walk-in aviary for both breeders and pets; this aviary is eight feet high, six feet long and six feet wide. Cockatoos spread their wings and have more need for exercise than Amazons and macaws; consequently the aviary must be roomy.

The aviary is supplied with two or three hollow logs for nesting and concealment (cockatoos love to conceal themselves in a getaway place from time to time). These logs are placed medium to high in the pen. Feeding pans are placed inside the door, which has a special opening to the outside. Since breeding cockatoos can become pugnacious during incubation, this arrangement of feeding pans allows for easy access and a minimum of disturbance.

This large cage is well suited for pet cockatoos. Notice the substantial perch which has been provided. Photo by Dr. Herbert R. Axelrod.

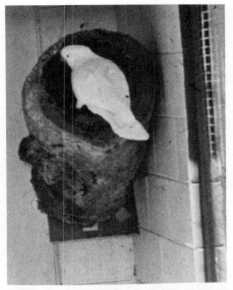

Breeding cockatoos need large quarters. *Right:* In this aviary a hollow log has been provided as a nesting site. *Below:* Here a large galvanized garbage can with a hole in it and a perch attached to it is used as a nest. Photo by Louise Van der Meid.

Such a large cage as this provides room for the cockatoo to exercise its wings, and the chain provides an outlet for the bird's predilection for chewing. Note the damage done to the roof when the bird was out of its cage. Photo by Glen S. Axelrod.

These feeding and watering pans can be placed at medium height within the aviary.

I prefer a black dirt base in most of the aviaries as the cockatoos not only get much good out of it in the form of minerals, but they also fluff their feathers in it for a dry bath. It is extremely good for them.

Our attempt at placing vegetation into the cockatoo aviaries was extremely unsuccessful. Like most parrots, cockatoos tend to completely denude all vegetation. They chew all of the wood to bits. In order to combat the chewing, many aviculturists have successfully used chain link fencing. It is advisable to place complete branches in the aviary just for chewing and to give the birds something to do. It is best to use apple tree branches, but I also use birch and pine. I have sometimes used oak with no problems, but since oak leaves are heavy with acid, care must be taken when providing them to your birds. Do not use cherry wood, as it is dangerous.

If you have a pet cockatoo, it is worthwhile to look for a very large cage suitable for a large macaw or a large monkey. Use nothing smaller. You will find that your cockatoo will be much happier in such a large cage. It is also advisable to place a very large, tough perch in the cage, both for resting and for chewing.

As you work with your cockatoo, it will be beneficial to take it out of the cage during certain periods of the day. Your cockatoo can flap its wings for more complete exercise.

In summation, I believe a large aviary is needed for the successful breeding of cockatoos. The birds need freedom to move about when they desire, and they need to be left undisturbed.

Although a mixture of different seeds may be your cockatoo's main fare, chunks and wedges of fruits should also be offered. Photo by Glen S. Axelrod.

Feeding the Cockatoo

The cockatoo, in my opinion, is the most fastidious of all the birds I have kept. They are extremely fussy in taking most foods as well as quite cautious before accepting any food. As tame and docile as many of my cockatoos are, they still prefer eating when we are not around.

When I purchase a new cockatoo, I worry more than with any other type of bird I might add to my aviaries. It seems that each time I do add a new cockatoo to the aviaries, there is a long period of time during which the bird seems to fast. In due time my uneasiness is overcome, since eventually they do start eating. More often than not they start with sunflower seeds, the universal parrot favorite.

When you purchase a cockatoo that has been imported, your chance of the bird beginning to eat quickly is much less than if you purchased from a breeder. The reason, of course, is that these imported cockatoos were fed with a wet rice mixture, which is quite different from what a breeder feeds his birds. It is very difficult to switch a bird from a specific diet to items that are very different. It is important to give a varied diet to your cockatoos to not only insure that they receive the necessary protein but also to be sure that they receive the fats that are necessary for maintaining a healthy body and for reproduction. I want to note that vitamins and minerals are extremely important for the maintenance of a healthy cockatoo also.

We tend to utilize four different food mixtures which are fed according to a particular schedule. Three days per week we feed a mixture that is our basic standby. We use 25% safflower seed (which costs about twice as much as sunflower seed), 25% sunflower seed (which contains many

Feeding dishes which are placed on a shelf or on the floor of an aviary should be heavy or weighted so that they are not easily tipped over. The dishes shown here are made of clay. Photo by Dr. Gerald R. Allen.

of the necessary fatty acids) and 10% monkey chow (which is not only nutritive and good for the cockatoos but also gives them something to chew on—it keeps them amused much of the time). We also add to this mixture 10% cracked corn, which we believe is needed by cockatoos more than any other kind of parrot. 5% of the total is a prepared pigeon feed which contains maple peas, corn, flax and hemp. The final addition to the mixture consists of a group of seeds: rape seed, oat groats, ground peanuts, red millet and white millet. This complete mixture is readily accepted by the cockatoos once they are well adjusted to our conditions. We generally feed this mixture on Monday, Wednesday and Friday.

On these same days we feed a fruit mixture in another dish. This fruit concoction is pre-cut on the previous Saturday and frozen until needed. We cut into small chunks various fruits: apples, pears, oranges, grapes, lemons, papayas and bananas. Before feeding, we insure that the entire amount is completely thawed.

On Tuesday and Thursday we feed a warm mixture. We start out with boiled rice, using both the cooked rice and the rice water. To this we add Purina dog chow and raisins. We feed this wet, sloppy concoction when it is warm. This is one of the feeding mixtures that our breeding cockatoos seem to love, perhaps for the ease they have in feeding it to their young. Anything that is uneaten by the end of the day, however, must be removed because a wet mixture such as this can become sour quite rapidly.

On Saturday and Sunday we have more time and prepare a baked concoction which our cockatoos have readily learned to enjoy. We vary the consistency of this mixture from time to time by putting various types of foods into it. We take cornmeal, eggs, buttermilk, ground monkey chow, honey and millet seed, and mix them well. This "batter" is then poured into baking pans and baked until done. When cooled but still warm, this is broken into chunks which are then fed to the birds. Seldom do we find a cockatoo that will not eat this "millet cake," as we call it.

In another dish we feed fresh canned corn off the cob. This is something nutritious that is relished by most birds.

There certainly are many ways to provide minerals for your cockatoos; one I utilize is clean sand from my own back yard. The cockatoos get much out of picking around in this sandy light soil. Another good system is to use ground oyster shell both in a special utensil within the aviary and soaked in water overnight. Then the water containing the minerals from the oyster shells can be used for their drinking purposes.

As aviculturists and pet owners today, we are fortunate in

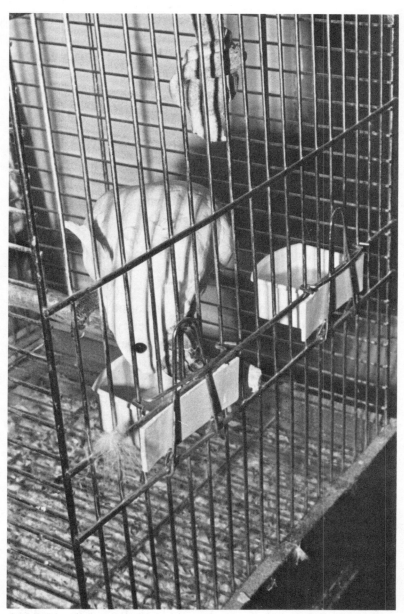

Attaching dishes directly to the bars of a cage allows easy access
for changing the water and refilling the food containers. Photo by
Dr. Herbert R. Axelrod.

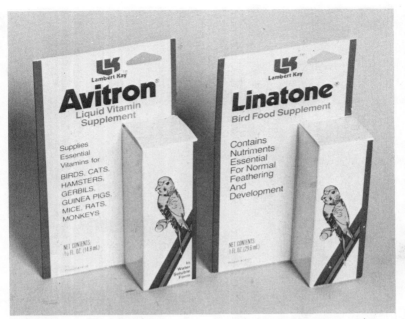

There are several fine vitamin supplements available in pet shops. Many of these may simply be added to the water normally provided for your bird.

that there now are liquid prepared vitamins which we can introduce into the birds' water. We constantly use this when we do not give the oyster shell water.

There are times when we feed raw apple wedges. We also rely heavily on certain greens, although we never feed lettuce and parsley. We do feed dandelion greens when they are in season and, depending on availability, endive, spinach, swiss chard and chicory at various other times of the year.

When you have healthy birds, feeding should be your most important concern. If you do not offer a complete diet, your birds will not reproduce for you; likewise, if you do not offer your pet a complete diet, you will not be able to train it as well.

This entrance to a nestbox used by a pair of Leadbeater cockatoos shows the extent of damage which can be inflicted by chewing. Photo by Louise Van der Meid.

Breeding the Cockatoo

One of the most interesting yet frustrating experiences for an aviculturist is the attempt to successfully breed and raise cockatoos. I have heard some aviculturists state that cockatoos breed like chickens; in other words, they are excellent breeders. I have also heard others speak of the difficult times they have had in rearing young cockatoos.

It has been established that cockatoos must be at least five or six years of age, depending on species, before they are ready to go into the nesting hole, lay the one or two eggs they normally produce, fully incubate them to term and then raise at least one baby.

If ever an aviculturist was adept at hand-raising young baby parrots, he must certainly be so when raising young cockatoos. In most cases cockatoos will lay two eggs, often several days apart. They generally begin incubating immediately. When the first chick hatches, they generally feed it quite well. However, on numerous occasions I have seen them pay little attention, if any, to the second chick. If not removed immediately for hand-feeding, it will most surely die. Not all cockatoos will neglect all their babies, as I have had at least two different pairs of lesser sulphur-crested cockatoos that have successfully raised all their babies each time. However, the usual turn of events ends in one lost baby and one healthy, well-cared-for baby.

Cockatoos most often lay two eggs, with two main exceptions: the lesser sulphur-crested cockatoo often lays three and the red-tailed black cockatoo lays one egg at each nesting. There are times when the funereal or yellow-tailed black cockatoo lays only one egg. (We must keep in mind, however, that the black cockatoos have not been bred in the United States.)

45

Galvanized garbage cans make fine nestboxes for such ardent chewers as cockatoos. Notice that several large perches are also provided for the pair. Photo by Frank Nothaft.

Once you select a pair of cockatoos for breeding and are sure they are of breeding age, then you must start to think about the type of nest box or nest hole to utilize. I have tried three different kinds, two of which have worked.

First, I attempted to use a grandfather clock style nest box. It was five feet high with a large opening about one-third of the way down. The hole was big enough for a large cockatoo to enter. A ladder type of climbing apparatus was used for the birds to climb down the inside of the nest box. The detrimental part of the use of this type of nest box is the constant chewing of wood by all cockatoos. On several occasions I have heard where chewed out bottoms of nest boxes have resulted in broken eggs on the floor of an aviary. I believe the saddest occasion was when an aviculturist friend of mine told me that his pair of Leadbeaters was sitting on two eggs. The next time I talked to him he indicated that the parents had chewed out the entire bottom of the nest box, thereby destroying the eggs. What a sad and terrifying loss!

The second type of nest box that I used was thick and hollow apple tree logs; other types of thick tree logs will also do well. They must be thick enough to prevent the cockatoos from chewing through the entire wood. I have had good success with these logs, especially when I have made sure that the entrance hole was high and that the adults had sufficient entry room.

The third nesting habitat I have used is a large garbage can with a hole made in the side. The cover is sealed on for top protection. Within each of the nest cavities I use shavings and black greenhouse dirt to cover the bottom to a depth of about three inches.

After the first entrance into the nesting box or log, it is interesting to note the splendid displays made by both the male and the female. I particularly note this in umbrella cockatoos. The male will spread out his wings to the maximum and hop along the branch or a perch and make several bows up and down to the female. He also utters a weird series of cackles that seldom is heard at any other time. The female crouches and flutters her wings constantly. After this display has continued for a while, copulation takes place. Most of these occurrences have been noted on early mornings or early evenings.

When the first egg is laid, it is generally the male cockatoo that does the incubating during the day; in the evening the female takes over. This does not occur in other members of the parrot family, with the exception of the cockatiel and a very few others.

When the adults are incubating, it is very important that feeding practices be changed by the addition of more protein. I try to do this in the form of meat; however, unlike Amazons and macaws which love meat and meat products, cockatoos just do not take meat with enjoyment. Occasionally a few will devour canned dog food, but their real high protein choice is various types of cheese. I also feed a lot of bread and milk with honey added. They particularly relish this treat when they are feeding their young.

I also increase the amount of fresh vegetables and fresh fruits, especially oranges and lemons as well as grapefruit, which they thoroughly enjoy. I give quite a lot of mashed cooked potatoes as well as numerous cooked sweet potatoes. They perhaps enjoy the cooked sweet potatoes most of all. Other products that I feed to breeding cockatoos include buttermilk, cottage cheese and whole wheat bread broken into bits.

If indeed you do have to hand-feed the baby the parents pay no attention to, it is important that you just give this baby a few drops of water for the first seventy-two hours, as he or she is living on the nutrients of the egg yolk. After this first seventy-two hour period you may make a mixture

The real beauty and appeal that this one-day-old umbrella cockatoo will develop as it matures is difficult to imagine right now. Photo by Frank Nothaft.

Baby cockatoos seem to be continuously hungry, and they do not hesitate to let their parents and you know about it. This is a thirteen-day-old greater sulphur-crested cockatoo. Photo by Frank Nothaft.

of oatmeal with apple sauce and bananas and add Avitron or some other type of bird vitamin. Also add one teaspoon of honey and cooked cream of wheat. We have had excellent luck with this formula when we have insured that it is given about every two hours during the first three weeks. After that period of time we add sunflower hearts that have been blended very well. We also increase the honey. During the next week we add blended meaty canned dog food. We feel that this needed protein does much to help the development of healthy bodies and a fine feather structure.

The breeding of various species and subspecies of cockatoos is still in its infancy. So little is known about many breeding characteristics of these birds. We must increase our knowledge—to prevent infertility, to insure that all chicks are raised to maturity and to even possibly increase the size of each clutch.

You may or may not want to wear gloves when you begin to train your cockatoo to climb onto your hand. Whichever you choose to do, the important thing to remember is that you want to gain your bird's trust. Photo by Dr. Herbert R. Axelrod.

Training Your Cockatoo

There are perhaps as many ways of training cockatoos as there are trainers. Everyone seems to have his or her favorite manner and type of training.

Whichever type of training procedure you employ, the training also might include using tidbits of the bird's favorite food as a reward for successful completion of a performance. Some people have also used other types of rewards; for example, head scratching is so enjoyed by some tamed birds that that is employed as a reward.

There are perhaps three different classes of cockatoos to train. First, one has the hand-raised baby that is already superbly trained and extremely tame. You are way ahead if you are fortunate enough to receive a cockatoo such as this. At this stage of training when much has already been done, one can begin training the young cockatoo to speak as well as to do various entertaining tricks.

The second type of cockatoo involves the bird that is only partially fearful of its owner. My suggestion is to take a large perch in order to begin stick training. Reach into the cage very slowly to see if the cockatoo will climb on and stay on. At first your bird might try to fly to another part of the cage, but do not give up; keep trying—cautiously. There are some trainers who prefer to use their hand, either with or without gloves, instead of a stick. I tend to believe in using bare hands. In time, with much patience, the cockatoo will surprise you by climbing onto your hand.

My cockatoos have generally taken small but nonpainful bites during the first training session; this is an indication that they are happy with the arrangement, but they are being cautious as well.

Above: Different people use different rewards when training their cockatoos. Some people (and birds) prefer to use food, some prefer scratching the head, and some prefer scratching under the wing. Photo by Kerry Donnelly. *Below:* Once a cockatoo feels confident sitting on your hand, the bird may start climbing up your arm in order to reach the highest possible place. Photo by Dr. Herbert R. Axelrod.

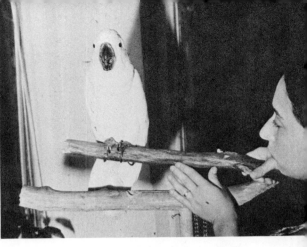

If your bird does not feel entirely comfortable with you, you can use a wooden perch to begin training and later use your hand in place of the perch. Photo by Dr. Herbert R. Axelrod.

The next step is to take the bird out of the cage on your hands to see if it indeed will remain or fly away to hit a window or a mirror. If it does fly away, make sure that it does not hit a window or a mirror; this is most dangerous and can result in a concussion.

In time your cockatoo will be at home sitting on your hand and will soon start walking up your arm to your shoulder—a parrot will always try to get to the highest possible position. By using certain types of taps, you can teach a cockatoo to raise and lower its crest. After another period of time you will note that your bird will be calm and more sure of itself. Soon it will be saying a few words, although a cockatoo will never be the talker that the African grey or some Amazons might be.

Finally, one may have an extremely wild and fearful older cockatoo that might have been caught in the wild. This bird must undergo a long series of sessions with the owner sitting by the cage constantly talking softly to alleviate the fear. Only when you can approach the cage without disturbing the cockatoo should you start opening the cage to develop closer contact. It is fun and also wonderfully exciting to have the ability to take a wild cockatoo and tame it. The result will be a lovable, docile bird that will give you not only much pride but also constant entertainment and satisfaction.

Although rarity of a bird should not play a role in a judge's decision, rarity does occasionally influence a decision. This is a rare hybrid between a rose-breasted cockatoo and a greater sulphur-crested cockatoo

Cockatoos In Exhibition

The excitement and fun of exhibiting at bird shows give one much pleasure. It is exciting to learn more about your cockatoo and to see just how the judging panel compares your bird to other cockatoos of the same species as well as to cockatoos and other parrots in the special award classes. Whether you are a pet owner or an aviculturist who breeds many cockatoos, you must begin planning for an exhibition months in advance of the show season.

Most shows begin in late September or early October and continue to late December. Occasionally one sees a show in early January. In addition, there are numerous summer fun shows that are smaller and set up for the benefit of novice pet owners and beginning breeders. These "feather shows" are very helpful as learning aids. They are called "feather shows" since most of the entrants are newly feathered young birds of the new season.

Most judges utilize several characteristics when reviewing a panel of cockatoos in exhibition. It is worthwhile to thoroughly understand each category. Your handling and treatment of your cockatoo during the weeks and months before an exhibition will greatly benefit both you and your bird on the day of the show.

Although there is no specific standard for a cockatoo in general, there is a standard as such for the parrot in general, as well as most exhibited birds. A general parrot judge has to know a tremendous amount about each type of parrot in order to properly judge each bird. For example, one must be able to differentiate between the top characteristics of a rose-breasted cockatoo and the top characteristics exhibited by a palm cockatoo. Consequently, the judge must have

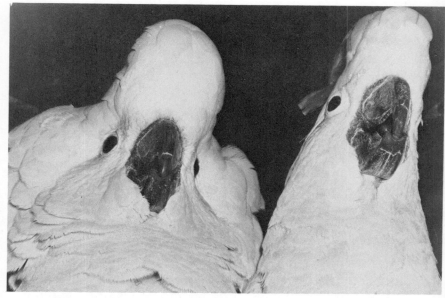

Of all the categories on which a cockatoo is judged, the one most affected by you is deportment—how the bird acts during the judging. This involves such things as whether or not the bird is flighty and whether or not it is excitable. A bird which raises its crest and fluffs out its feathers will probably not do as well in the judging as one which has a calm and composed appearance. Photo by Glen S. Axelrod.

certain categories in mind. These are conformation, condition, deportment, color, pattern and rarity. Condition is most important since it includes general condition of the cockatoo as well as feather condition. One must look for a bird that may be too thin or too fat. One must also look for dullness of color as part of condition. Feathers must be perfect; there cannot be bad fringes on the tail endings or the primary and secondary wing feathers. A judge must therefore ask himself several questions. Are wing and tail feathers frayed from the bird hitting the bars of the cage too frequently? Are the feathers bright or dull? Does the plumage lie close and smooth to the body? Are the legs and feet clean or scaly? Needless to say, they should be smooth and clean. The beak must not be overgrown. Likewise, claws must be trimmed and not so abnormally long as to get caught in caging or other material. A missing or crooked toe is not as important as many people try to make it unless there is strong competition or unless the cockatoo is in the finals of judging for Best Parrot or Best In Show.

To prevent fringing of tails and wings, and to prevent getting docked for long claws and overgrown beaks, you should constantly be aware of the condition of the cockatoo in question. Keep the beak and claws properly trimmed. Maintain your cockatoo in a cage large enough to prevent the fringing of tail and wings. Make sure your bird gets used to the cage in which you plan to show it. Spray your bird daily with a fine cold water spray. This spraying will do more for feather condition than you will fully realize.

Conformation is the next major category to consider. The judge and the exhibitor must be completely aware of all the chief characteristics of the specific cockatoo being judged. For example, does this particular cockatoo have a sufficiently sized crest in comparison to the others exhibited at that particular show? Is the tail carried too high or too low in comparison to the others exhibited? Is the line of carriage from the head down the back to the tail straight or broken? If it is broken, a bad defect is obvious. Conformation must weigh quite heavily in overall number of points, as must condition.

Deportment is perhaps most affected by you, the exhibitor. This involves the action of the bird during the actual time of judging. Does the bird travel all over the cage during the judging, or does it stand perfectly still on the perch so the judge can readily look it over for all characteristics? A bird that is flighty or one which will not properly perch for a judge may well be put down for lack of deportment.

Color and pattern are important but not as important as condition and conformation. Of course, dullness of color or

Left: Unlike this cockatoo, a show cockatoo must be in good feather—no fringes, no frays, no dull color and no untidiness. Photo courtesy of Vogelpark Walsrode. *Below:* Trimming the claws (and beak) is important for any cockatoo, but it is especially important to prevent losing points with a show bird. Photo by Dr. Herbert R. Axelrod.

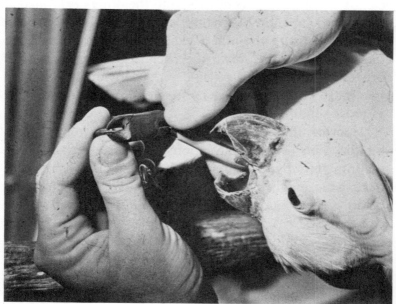

brightness of color has already been discussed under condition. With color and pattern in mind, one could ask how bright is the yellow in the crest of a particular sulphur-crested cockatoo? How bright are the ear patches on the sulphur-crested cockatoo? Is the pattern in the crest of the Leadbeater cockatoo distinct and broad in comparison to other Leadbeaters at this show? All colors should be as clear and as rich as possible. Likewise, patterns should be as definitive as possible. Judges should guard against being prejudiced about brilliant colors. A well-conformed Goffin's cockatoo which is in good condition should get as much notice and chance as a well-conformed rose-breasted cockatoo which is in good condition.

Many judges stress the rarity of a bird when judging. For the final judging, they may take two birds that are equal in every way, such as a gang-gang cockatoo and a lesser sulphur-crested cockatoo, and give the final prize to the gang-gang simply because it is the rarer of the two cockatoos. I do not believe that rarity should play a part in the overall judging and, consequently, I do not use this subject in my judging. I do, however, honor those judges who utilize this system.

Finally, many judges take into consideration the type of facilities an exhibitor has provided for the bird. Does this bird have sufficient room to turn about in the exhibition cage? Is the perch too big or too small for the feet of the cockatoo being exhibited? Can the judge sufficiently see the bird being exhibited, or is it in a cage which is much too dark? These are questions the judge may have to ask.

When preparing to exhibit your cockatoo, you must secure a copy of the show catalog, perhaps much in advance of the show, in order to read the rules of that show. You should then look for the class in which you wish to enter your cockatoo. Chances are that in properly classified shows there will be several classes of cockatoos. If you have a lesser sulphur-crested cockatoo to exhibit, hopefully there will be a class for lesser sulphur-crested cockatoos. General-

Although there are no specific requirements concerning size, color and so forth of a show cage, the cage in which you show your bird is often taken into consideration when your bird is judged. It is up to you to provide facilities of adequate size with good perches, facilities which do not show your bird in a poor light literally or figuratively. Photo by Louise Van der Meid.

Cockatoos often preen themselves, and each other, to keep their feathers in good order. You can help retain your bird's good feather condition by daily spraying it with cold water.

ly there are awards for first, second and third place in each class. If you are lucky enough to defeat the other lessers and get a blue ribbon for first, then your bird is eligible to compete with the other first place cockatoos of different kinds for a special award of Best Cockatoo. If your lesser sulphur-crested cockatoo defeats the best greater, the best rose-breasted, the best Moluccan and so on as Best Cockatoo, you will get either a trophy, a special rosette or both.

The Best Cockatoo is then eligible to compete against the Best Lory, Best Cockatiel, Best Rosella and so on for Best of the South Pacific Parrots. This winner goes on to compete with Best Afro-Asian Parrot, Best South American Parrot and Best Mutation Parrot for the Best Parrot In Show. This winner is then eligible to compete for the Supreme Best Bird In Show against the Best Canary, Best Finch, Best Dove, Best Softbill and Best Mule or Hybrid. One bird emerges the victor over all.

Exhibiting a bird is a thrilling experience for any pet owner or aviculturist. It is worthwhile to exhibit, and you and your bird may just come away from the show with top honors!

There are several cockatoos which should at least be considered threatened in their native areas. The red-tailed or Banksian cockatoo is one such threatened cockatoo. Photo by Louise Van der Meid.

The Endangered Species

In order to insure the continued well-being of many species of wild fauna and flora, the U.S. Department of the Interior promulgates rules and regulations in accordance with the Convention on International Trade in Endangered Species. There are no endangered cockatoos currently listed on the endangered list, although there are many cockatoos that cannot be exported from Australia due to Australian export laws initiated in 1959. This is why many of the black cockatoos are so rare in this country. In addition, other types of cockatoos, such as the great black palm cockatoo from New Guinea, are considered threatened and so must come into this country with a special permit. (The mistake too frequently made is that once some of these birds do enter this country without the special permit, too many people are much too anxious to destroy the birds rather than attempt to check them for health and to find a home for them in a zoo or other avicultural institution.

The following list includes the cockatoos that I consider threatened.

Red-tailed black cockatoo
Yellow-tailed black cockatoo
White-tailed black cockatoo
Great black palm cockatoo
Slender-billed cockatoo
Gang-gang cockatoo

I would strongly consider adding the Goffin's cockatoo to the list if the islands on which it used to thrive continue to become ravaged for their lumber by the forestry divisions of various countries.

Many of the land areas from which cockatoos originate have been de-forested or in some other way encroached upon by civilization. Although breeding in captivity is especially important for the survival of cockatoos already threatened, captive breeding is important for the perpetuation of all cockatoos. Photo by Glen S. Axelrod.

The slender-billed cockatoo, also known as the blood-stained cockatoo and the long-billed corella, is the rarest white cockatoo. Photo by Louise Van der Meid.

One must consider breeding all types of cockatoos to insure their continued survival, for it will not be the breeders of birds that will endanger the species, but the encroachment on the birds' environments by civilization.

Preventing accidents and ailments is usually far easier than their treatment. Two obvious preventive measures (necessities) for the health and well-being of any bird are cleanliness and a good diet. Photo by Dr. Herbert R. Axelrod.

Preventive Medicine

Every bird owner should always prevent the occurrence of diseases and parasite infestations in cage and aviary birds. Preventive medicine is most important; if followed correctly one can achieve standards that will save much stress and suffering in the future.

The most important aspect of preventive veterinary medicine deals with the acquisition of new birds; you must always isolate new birds for at least thirty days, and sixty days would be better. During the isolation period, you must watch for signs of distress, weakness and poor appetite. It is always wise to immediately start feeding a high protein, high vitamin diet. I suggest the addition of vitamins to the diet. Aviculturists can feel quite fortunate, since certain commercial forms of multi-vitamin preparations are readily available in pet shops; these preparations provide the necessary A, B, C, D and E vitamins.

Vitamin A is required for the normal development of bone structure, but in the new cagebird it is especially valuable in building an immunity against dread diseases. For this reason, giving extra vitamin A according to directions on the package is advisable for new birds. Vitamin A is unstable, so it is important not to depend upon its provision in a food that has been stored for a long time; the vitamin A content will have disappeared. I suggest feeding a good supply of apples and carrots for vitamin A provision.

Vitamin D aids in the absorption and disposition of calcium and phosphorus. A deficiency of this vitamin will cause rickets in young birds. Multivitamin supplements

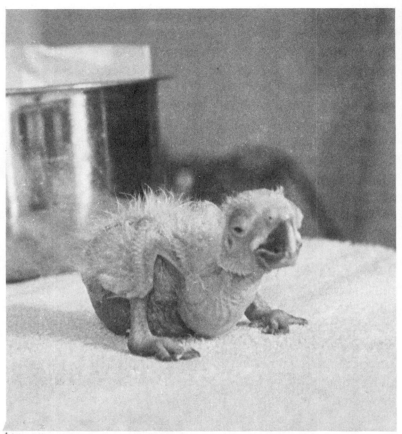

If you have a very young cockatoo, start it off right by making sure it receives a well-balanced diet, one rich in vitamins and other nutrients. Photo by Manolo Guevara.

will prevent rickets in young birds if you have success in hatching them.

Vitamin E is important in the reproduction performance of the female cockatoo and normal fertility in the mature male. It should best be given to cagebirds in the form of multiple vitamins. However, I do like to give my cockatoos vitamin E capsules; they love to crack them open for the vitamin oil.

There are many vitamins in the vitamin B complex; all are important in preventive medicine. Vitamin B is required for growth and hatchability. Cockatoos can readily receive plenty of B from multiple vitamins as well as from whole wheat bread. They seem to enjoy the wheat bread very much.

When you purchase a bird, make sure that you select a *healthy* bird. If you purchase your bird from a breeder rather than from a pet shop, choose a breeder who exhibits and has had long standing breeding pairs. In either case, when you start with a healthy bird, you will find that you are ahead, because it is a fact that it is easier to maintain a healthy bird than nurse a sick bird back to health.

Your prime sources of birds will be pet shops and private breeders. I believe that, in general, breeders will have healthier stock than pet shops, especially if the breeders have long experience with birds. At the same time, many birds sold in pet shops have been obtained from private

To make sure your cockatoo gets enough vitamins in its diet, you can purchase different supplements. These supplements can be either fed directly to the bird or placed in the food or water. Follow the directions given on the product.

Get to know your bird and its habits. Be alert and make note of any abnormal behavior; it may be a sign of an ailment which can be prevented from developing into something serious. Photo by Dr. Herbert R. Axelrod.

breeders and therefore share whatever advantages such stock offers. Additionally, not everyone can get into contact with a private breeder locally, and most people do not wish to go through all the trouble of purchasing by mail.

Regardless of where you buy a bird, make sure the bird looks alert and not fluffed up. Stay away from a bird that constantly holds its head under its wing with fluffed up feathers. You may well be purchasing a sick bird that soon dies, and there are few sellers that will replace a bird that you have had over two days.

Always watch the droppings of new birds. They should be solid green and white. If they become loose or yellowish green, you should go to an avian veterinarian immediately for advice and treatment. If your bird gets fluffed up and listless, immediately place it in a high heat area, preferably 90°F.

When your cockatoo shows slight signs of respiratory problems, place the recommended dosage of antibiotic powder in the drinking water. Use only tetracycline or Achromycin. Do not use chloromycetin.

Another wonder drug that has proved successful to me is the use of Vicks Vaporub on the nostrils. Keep in mind that in preventive medicine you may have to use some medicine. You should view your cockatoo at least three times per day for any changes in the bird's disposition, ruffled or fluffed up feathers, drowsiness, restlessness, pasty vent area, loss of appetite and abnormal droppings. These changes should be apparent immediately, and with luck you can prevent your cockatoo from suffering any illness for years.

This bird is suffering from a congenital condition which causes it to look as if it has been feather-plucked. Photo by Steve Kates.

Common Ailments and Diseases

Keep in mind that warmth is the important element in the treatment of a sick bird. Remember that when a bird is sick, the minimum temperature to use is 85°F. Any sick bird should be housed and given treatment in this heat until it has recovered. Only then should the temperature be gradually reduced.

VITAMIN DEFICIENCY

Small yellow pustules will occur in the mouth, and on autopsy of a lost bird these yellow pustules will be seen on the esophagus. Treat with vitamin A as soon as pustules appear. You should add multi-vitamins to a cockatoo's diet at all times to prevent occurrences such as this.

ASPERGILLOSIS

This is caused by a fungus called *Aspergillus fumigatus* which invades the throat, the air sacs and the lungs of the bird. Prevention is by feeding only clean seed. Don't let the seed get moldy, and do not use moldy hay or straw. This is a carrier of the organism. Cockatoos with this disease make a wheezing sound when breathing; they appear to have deep, severe respiratory difficulty. There is no completely adequate treatment once a bird has this disease.

BUMBLEFOOT

This results from a staphylococcus infection. Drainage and then treatment with antibiotics will be successful.

Bumblefoot only occasionally occurs in cockatoos that are recently imported.

BRONCHITIS

Serious nasal discharge occurs, accompanied by a severe respiratory difficulty. The cockatoo becomes depressed and fluffs its feathers. The bird will eat fairly well during this bad period. Treat with Terramycin or Aureomycin in water. Spray cortisone into the nostrils. Apply Vicks Vaporub on the nostrils. Place in heat as usual. You may also unplug the nostrils with a toothpick and steam with melted Vicks thirty minutes per day.

CATARACTS

This is a hereditary disease of the eyes which is carried on a dominant gene. It is best to dispose of breeders that pass this trait on to their offspring. This is seen only occasionally in cockatoos.

CHILLS

If taken to warmth immediately, almost all birds with simple chill will definitely recover within twelve hours—if put in a temperature of 85 to 90°F.

CONVULSIONS

On occasion, one will see a cockatoo in a convulsion. Almost always the convulsion is associated with a vitamin B deficiency. Prevent it first by administration of liquid multi-vitamins. Two milliliters of thiamine hydrochloride daily will prevent further convulsions.

CONJUNCTIVITIS

This condition occurs as a watery discharge from the eye, and the eyelids may become swollen to the extent that temporary blindness occurs. Immediately apply an antibiotic ointment containing only an approved antibiotic. Do not use streptomycin, which is dangerous to birds.

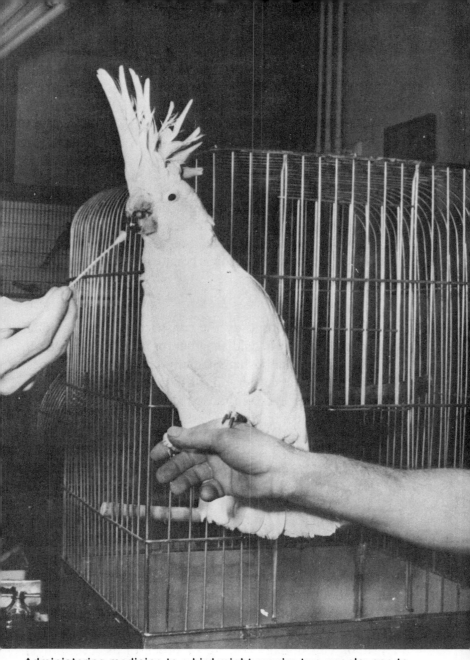

Administering medicine to a bird might require two people: one to hold the bird and one to give the medicine. This citron-crested cockatoo is getting a swabbing. A Wide World photo.

CROP BINDING

This occurs in young cockatoos more often than in adults. You should manipulate the crop to dislodge the binding. Give mineral oil by mouth; this will ease the dislodged material to the lower esophagus, then into the proventriculus and on to the gizzard. This occurs more frequently in hand-raised baby cockatoos.

CROP SICKNESS

A bird with crop sickness continuously vomits a watery fluid. You must distinguish this behavior from normal actions between breeding cockatoos. Acute cases can be treated with Kaopectate or bicarbonate of soda. Do not feed any gravel for a few days.

EGG BINDING

Egg binding is caused by the constriction of the oviduct and goes along with cold weather or sudden changes in temperature. Cockatoo hens usually come out of the nest and will sit in a corner all fluffed up. The wings are drooped and the eyes are closed. In most cases complete recovery will occur if you place the cockatoo in 90°F. heat. In just a few hours the egg will be laid. Hens that become egg bound should be rested for at least sixty days. A prevention that has been successful for this author is one teaspoonful of gin in a half pint of water while the birds are laying.

ENTERITIS

This is actually an inflammation of the intestines. Causes are many; it could have a psychological cause such as extreme nervousness and excitement. Changes in diet or in environment or vascular blood changes within the intestine will also cause enteritis. It might also have a nutritional cause, such as too much fruit, too many greens, deficiency of grit or coprophagy (eating of other birds' droppings). Various infections will cause enteritis. Some of the worst are caused by salmonella, pasteurella and streptococcus.

Symptoms include abnormally green and watery droppings which may be bloody. The feathers are ruffled and the cockatoo is listless. Affected birds often have a pasty vent and wet feathers. When studying the droppings of cockatoos with enteritis you should pay attention to the following colors and conditions:

Yellow to yellow green — infectious enteritis
Brown, dry, scanty — pneumonia
Yellow with blood — psittacosis
Grayish white or watery — coccidiosis
Gray and gummy — nephritis or kidney disease

When you treat the bird, you should consider all types of enteritis to be infectious. Treat with broad-spectrum antibiotics such as Terramycin or Aureomycin. B complex vitamins are also necessary as well as additional fluids. Other home treatments include boiled rice water, which is extremely helpful. You can also boil three teabags for three minutes, let them steep and then let the cockatoo drink after the tea has cooled.

OVERGROWN BEAK

In older cockatoos the upper mandible often grows too long and becomes distorted. It also may cross the lower mandible. You must take great care in trimming the beak. The best instrument is a dog claw clipper in conjunction with a sharp pair of scissors.

OVERGROWN CLAWS

Luckily this condition does not always affect the cockatoo. If the condition does occur, you can hold the claw in a good light and cut it very carefully with dog claw clippers. Make sure you clip below the blood vessel. Once in a while you might get a bleeder; if you do, you're in trouble. If bleeding occurs, use flour or cornstarch on the claw. If it continues to bleed, secure the services of a veterinarian experienced in avian problems.

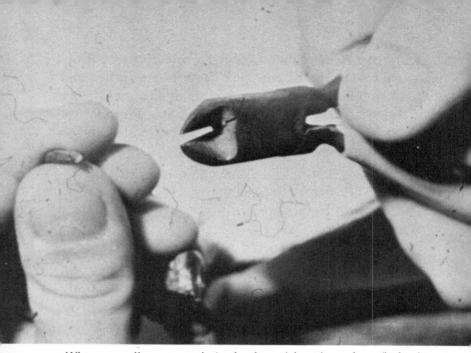

When you clip your cockatoo's claws (above) or wings (below), you must be very careful not to clip too much; you might hit a blood vessel. If you are at all unsure about the procedure, have an experienced individual show you how to do it. Photo by Dr. Herbert R. Axelrod.

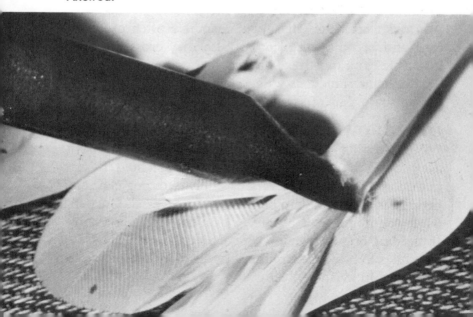

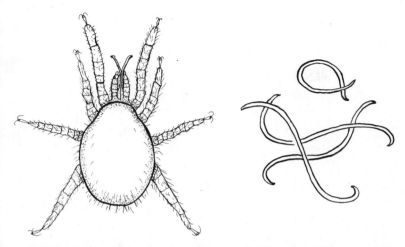

Parasites can debilitate your bird and can lead to the bird's death if they are not dealt with promptly. A veterinarian can best help to determine which parasite might be troubling your bird and how the parasite can be eliminated. *Above left:* a mite, an external parasite. *Above right:* roundworms, internal parasites.

INTERNAL PARASITES

Occasionally cockatoos will develop intestinal roundworms. Roundworm ova can be detected in the droppings by microscopic study. Liquid piperazine is the drug of choice—two teaspoons to a half pint of water.

In summation, you must consider the following:
1. Preventive measures will pay off.
2. If you notice that your bird is "off," place it in a heated area or in a hospital cage with a temperature of 85 to 90°F.
3. My favorite treatments which have cured many birds are Vicks Vaporub on the nares and Terramycin powder in the drinking water.
4. If you have real difficulty, consult your veterinarian. I have merely mentioned a few conditions seen in practice and experience in bird breeding populations.

Macaws are large parrots that originate in South America. Eclectus parrots (an eclectus is shown next to the macaw with upraised wings) are native to the Australia/New Guinea region. Both types of parrot are kept as pets. Photo by Kerry V. Donnelly.

CLASSIFICATION

Classification of Parrots

When considering the cockatoo as one major member of a large order or group of parrots, one must keep in mind a systematic approach in the overall classification of parrots.

I like to classify parrots first as three major geographical groups.

A) The south Pacific group involves all hookbills that originate from the Indonesia area through the south Pacific islands including New Guinea, one of the largest islands in the world, to New Zealand and Australia.

B) The Afro-Asian group covers all African species as well as Asian species, including India but excluding Indonesia.

C) Finally, the South American group includes not only the South American parrots but also those from North and Central America as well as the Caribbean islands.

Keeping in mind this classification, we then can move to ten subgroups.

1) True parrots include hookbills from all three geographical areas—worldwide. All true parrots have generally bulky bodies and squared-off tails; the tails often are short.

2) Parakeets, also worldwide in distribution, are elongated in body with an elongated tail. Parakeets do not have an eye ring, which would consist of a denuded feather ring about the eyes.

Jardine's parrot is native to Africa. It is a rare bird which looks like a miniature Amazon parrot. Photo by Harry V. Lacey.

3) The lories, only from the south Pacific distribution, are similar to the true parrots with a bulky body and squared-off tail, but with a tongue adapted for manipulating flowers for nectar. The tongue ends in many papillae.

4) The lorikeets look much like the parakeets with an elongated body and tail, but with the papillae of the tongue adapted for obtaining nectar. These likewise are in the south Pacific distribution.

5) The macaws, strictly South American representatives, are generally very large, having a very large bulky body with a very long tail. Miniatures are even larger than most parakeets. The main feature, however, is the fascinating bare facial patch.

6) The conures, also of the South American distribution, are halfway between the macaws and the parakeets. The bare patch does not exist; however, a bare ring about the eye does exist. With an elongated body and tail, the birds are smaller than most macaws. Certain true parrots also have bare eye patches; this includes some of the Amazons.

7) The lovebirds, strictly from Africa, are miniature true parrots, six to nine inches in length, with a bulky little body and a short square tail.

8) The parrotlets are even smaller true parrots found worldwide in distribution.

9) The cockatiel is a bird with a small elongated body and with an elongated tail; it also displays a crest. It is found only in Australia.

10) Finally, the cockatoos are large birds with a bulky body and generally a long squared-off tail; they always have a crest. They are all south Pacific birds.

Umbrella cockatoos are large white cockatoos with backward-curving crests. They are very plentiful and are easily bred in captivity. Photo by Kerry Donnelly.

Cockatoo Species

UMBRELLA COCKATOO
Cacatua alba

One of the most plentiful cockatoos is found on several islands northwest of New Guinea including the large island of Halmahera and the heavily bird-populated island of Obi; it is also numerous in Indonesia, where it was introduced years ago. This cockatoo, *Cacatua alba,* is the splendid umbrella or white cockatoo with a fabulous large erectile crest which swerves back over the head toward the back of the neck.

This large cockatoo, which is about eighteen inches long, is completely white in color, including the crest, but with a yellow suffusion under the wings and under the tail. The beak is large and strong with grayish black markings. It has been said by certain aviculturists that umbrella cockatoos will breed like chickens; I tend to occasionally believe it since my experiences have proven successful in breeding this species of cockatoo.

My two pairs of umbrella cockatoos are particularly interesting in their mannerisms and breeding habits. I have watched "Umbie," our majestic male, in a complete courtship display to his mate "Umbina." Umbie spreads his wings to the greatest extent, dancing on the perch at the same time. He bobs his head up and down, emitting a sharp, distinct call—as if to say, "This is my kingdom." Strangely, the female sits contented with little or no apparent emotion until the time of copulation.

One time I was in need of additional space so I added a young umbrella male to the aviary housing Umbie and Umbina. Although Umbie did not fight with the young male, he went through a similar ritual, emitting loud screeches. Surprisingly, the young male kept clear of both adults.

When I began to attempt breeding umbrella cockatoos, I utilized for nesting sites some beautiful wine kegs I had purchased at a fabulous price from a flea market. Within weeks the cockatoos had chewed the entire wine keg to bits, leaving only the steel rings surrounding the kegs. (Wood is highly necessary for umbrella cockatoos, not for nesting but for chewing.) I thereafter used galvanized garbage cans, cutting a hole in the side and inserting a perch. These were never chewed by the umbrella cockatoos.

My two pairs of umbrellas are both active breeders and very good parents, at least initially. It is noteworthy to mention that two white eggs are always in the clutch. I have had extremely good luck in hatching both chicks each time, and it was interesting to see the male incubating during the day, with the female taking over at night.

In comparison to lesser sulphur-crested cockatoos, with which I had no problems with the parents raising the young, my umbrellas seem to be very good parents to one chick but frequently pay little attention to the second chick. The second chick would often have been lost if I had not taken it out of the nest for hand-feeding. It became apparent that if I wanted to save both chicks, I did have to hand-feed one of them.

I overcame this problem by introducing canned dog food (heavy with meat) to the diet of the parents. Since this change was introduced, my success concerning the adults taking care of the second baby has been somewhat improved. I believe that a lack of protein in the diet created a condition in the parents whereby they could only suitably feed and raise one baby.

My experiences also indicate that baby umbrellas fledge

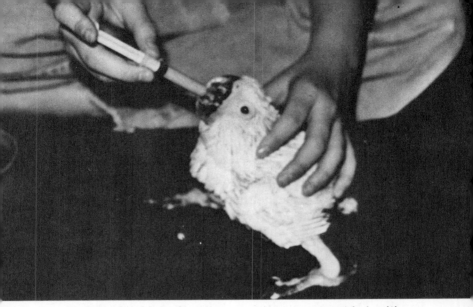

This six-week-old umbrella cockatoo is being hand-fed with a syringe. Photo by Jo Cooper.

fairly slowly—ten weeks generally for my birds. Feather condition until the first molt is very bad due to the excessive moving around in the nest for so long a period.

Umbrella cockatoos are delightful to have around. Although Umbie is an ideal breeder, he is also an excellent pet. Daren, our son, carries Umbie around on his arm. This bird loves to raise his crest, particularly if he is being shown to strangers. There are very many umbrella cockatoos imported into the United States each year, mostly from Indonesia. With the possible exception of the lesser sulphur-crested cockatoo, it appears that the umbrella is seen most often in the U.S.

Like most cockatoos, umbrellas are fairly poor eaters. They enjoy sunflower seeds, corn on the cob and apples in the aviary; I literally have to force other foods on them. They dislike people watching them eat. I also often see them eating at a distance. Even when I approach them (and many of them are hand-tame), they hesitate to eat.

DUCORP'S COCKATOO
Cacatua ducorps

For a bird that is very common in the Solomon Islands, east of New Guinea in the south Pacific, the Ducorp's cockatoo, *Cacatua ducorps*, is virtually unseen and unheard of in the United States. There may be a few Ducorp's cockatoos hidden away in an aviary or two somewhere, but in recent years I have neither seen nor read of any in existence in this country. In the early part of 1974, there also were no red-vented cockatoos in the United States; however, by 1976 they were imported in great numbers. Today there are very many red-vented cockatoos in zoos, aviaries and private collections. Perhaps the possibility exists that Ducorp's cockatoo will appear at import stations in the future.

I recall seeing two Ducorp's cockatoos about thirty years ago in a private collection. At that time I was capable of differentiating them from the lesser sulphur-crested cockatoos which were also part of the collection. In those times the subject of breeding cockatoos, or any type of parrot except budgies and a few cockatiels, was not even considered. Even the cockatiel was considered difficult to breed. I had a friend in Minnesota who had tremendous luck breeding budgies but was just getting started in cockatiels, with little success.

The Ducorp's cockatoo is characterized by a general body plumage color of white. The undersides of the wing and tail feathers are suffused with yellow. The lores are always white. Occasionally one sees a few pink feathers on the crown; less occasionally one sees pink feathers scattered sparsely on the breast. There are a few more pink feathers on the cheeks. The eye ring is dark blue and circular. Both the bill and the legs are gray. The eyes of the male are black, while the female's eyes are reddish brown.

This is a cockatoo to watch for. At the rate various parrot-type birds are being imported into this country, one may soon see a number of Ducorp's cockatoos in stock at various pet shops and importer facilities.

GREATER SULPHUR-CRESTED COCKATOO
Cacatua galerita galerita

The elite of all cockatoos, the greater sulphur-crested cockatoo is the most beautiful and aristocratic. The greater, as the name implies, is about a third larger than the lesser sulphur-crested cockatoo, ranging from twenty to twenty-two inches in length, but the bill on the lesser appears relatively larger than the bill on the larger greater sulphur-crested.

Cacatua galerita galerita has a generally white body plumage with pale yellow ear coverts and strong yellow shadings under the wings and tail. This magnificent bird appears well proportioned; I have never seen one in poor feather. As with other cockatoos, the sexes can be determined by standard eye color. The bill color is light gray.

Cacatua galerita galerita comes only from Australia, particularly the southern and southeastern parts. Since Australia has banned the export of all birds and mammals, the greater sulphur-crested cockatoo is extremely rare in the United States. Those in existence are either old birds or progeny of these birds.

My family acquired a fantastic, most attractive greater sulphur-crested cockatoo with a splendid history some years ago. "Josephine," as she is called, is a fine specimen. She is extremely tame and can readily be handled by my son Daren. She is so well mannered that she will not bite. Josephine's history goes back twenty-five years; as a young bird, she was purchased during the 1950's with a group of five other *Cacatua galerita galerita* from a well-known New York importer. One owner had her in a superb collec-

The greater sulphur-crested cockatoo is a magnificent bird; it has a very impressive forward-curving crest and a large wing span. Photo by Louise Van der Meid.

tion—until we acquired her. Unfortunately, her first owners did not have an interest in breeding. If they had, they might have had significant results since not only do they own greaters, but they also maintain lessers and three other species, Leadbeaters, great black palms and galahs. It is breathtaking to visit with these interesting people, since their collection far exceeds anything I have.

Josephine loves carrots and endive as well as raw white onions. Interestingly though, she refuses to eat if we watch her. We must be quite distant before she will attempt to eat. I have found in my experiences with cockatoos that almost all of them will react the same way. They may take a peanut or an apple from one's hand, but they will not eat in the presence of a human. It is well known among many cockatoo breeders that the eating habits of this major class of parrots is poor. They do not eat as readily and heartily as

Even with the crest not extended, the greater sulphur-crested cockatoo has an aristocratic appearance. Photo by Ann Krausse.

Amazons, conures or macaws. Many of them are very fussy eaters. It is most difficult to find foods that are great favorites of cockatoos in general.

Josephine is a quiet bird, yet we know she is around. She is seldom noisy. I strongly feel that most cockatoos in my collection of breeders are very quiet.

Some friends of mine, Gary and Janet Lilienthal, own a fabulous pair of male *Cacatua galerita galerita*. These are truly outstanding greaters; their names are "Wild" and "Crazy," but I don't particularly think that they are wild and crazy. In fact, they seem very well mannered.

If Australia were to ever open its doors to exportation, aviculturists in the United States and elsewhere would certainly be grateful, especially for the opportunity to acquire a magnificent greater sulphur-crested cockatoo.

ELEONORA COCKATOO
Cacatua galerita eleonora

Another greater sulphur-crested cockatoo, *Cacatua galerita eleonora,* is often called by many importers and brokers the medium sulphur-crested cockatoo. This cockatoo is a beautiful bird, large and well balanced, but is about three inches smaller than *Cacatua galerita galerita*. I shall still refer to this species as a greater sulphur-crested cockatoo since there are only two major differences from the nominate race. One involves the smaller size, the other the geographical origin.

This subspecies is found only in the Aru islands off Indonesia. The general body plumage is white. Ear coverts are light yellow. There is a yellow shading under the wings and tail. The beak is similar to *Cacatua galerita galerita* in that it is not too large. (Certain lesser sulphur-crested cockatoos have enormous bills—much larger than the bills of this subspecies of greater sulphur-crested cockatoo.)

During the early 1970's, *Cacatua galerita eleonora* was virtually unheard of in the United States. Importers seldom had many cockatoos for sale with the exception of a few lessers. In 1977, a great surge of so-called medium sulphur-crested cockatoos emerged on the scene. Many of these birds were various subspecies of *Cacatua sulphurea;* however, many were also *Cacatua galerita eleonora.*

I have mixed feelings on the terminology involving "medium cockatoos" that has hit the world of birds. Certainly when one is purchasing a cockatoo or a group of cockatoos (and many are purchased sight unseen), one wants to know specifically which subspecies he is getting. If a greater is advertised, are we disillusioned if we receive an Eleonora or a lesser with larger morphological characteristics? If a medium is listed on importer and broker lists, will you receive a *Cacatua sulphurea* or a *Cacatua galerita eleonora?*

Therefore, although a true medium sulphur-crested cockatoo doesn't exist taxonomically, those persons involved in the distribution and selling of cockatoos must properly outline just what the eventual customer will receive. Even with that, I know of certain persons who have purchased greater sulphur-crested cockatoos thinking they would receive a *C. galerita galerita* (although they are virtually impossible to secure) and received *Cacatua galerita eleonora,* still indeed a greater! I have also witnessed persons ordering medium sulphur-crested cockatoos thinking they would receive an Eleonora only to find they had received a larger lesser sulphur-crested cockatoo. In early 1979 a friend of mine purchased a medium sulphur-crested cockatoo from a broker with the idea that he would get a large lesser sulphur-crested cockatoo. To his delight he received a beautiful, large Eleonora.

There is no doubt that these Eleonoras are tremendous birds of great beauty. Most of those I have seen have been in extraordinary feather.

We have only seen the Eleonora imported in the late 1970's. In the current absence of *Cacatua galerita galerita,* they make an excellent replacement. As long as Australia maintains its ban, only a handful of *Cacatua galerita galerita* will enter the United States. Meanwhile, hopefully many breeders and aviculturists will work with and broaden the appearance of the Eleonora.

FITZROY GREATER SULPHUR-CRESTED COCKATOO
Cacatua galerita fitzroyi

Named after the Fitzroy River in northern Australia is another of the greater sulphur-crested cockatoos. This one is found in northern and western Australia; again we seldom see this subspecies due to the export regulations of Australia. Actually we see fewer *Cacatua galerita fitzroyi* than we do the nominate race, *Cacatua galerita galerita.*

The Fitzroy cockatoo is from one to two inches smaller than *C. galerita galerita;* there is less yellow on the ear coverts and under the wings and tail. The major difference is in the eye ring. The Fitzroy has a very pale blue ring around the eye, while *C. galerita galerita* has a white eye ring. This pale blue eye ring should not be confused with the brilliant blue eye ring of the blue-eyed cockatoo, *Cacatua ophthalmica.* Another morphological characteristic of the Fitzroy is displayed in the bill; it has a much broader bill than *Cacatua galerita galerita.*

Since literally no members of this subspecies are imported, there are very few specimens in evidence in the United States. Gary and Janet Lilienthal did own a Fitzroy for a long time—until its sudden death. Bill Feloni has a pair in his Michigan aviaries; this pair has been successful in breeding, almost always insuring Bill two chicks twice per year.

While visiting the Los Angeles Zoo in the summer of

1978, I noted a large aviary with about 60 to 70 large cockatoos. These birds had apparently been seized from an importer by the Fish and Game Department of the Department of the Interior. It was interesting for me to note the different species and subspecies involved. I did see a few Fitzroy individuals as well as blue-eyed cockatoos and umbrella cockatoos. *Cacatua galerita galerita* was also represented. This was a beautiful array of cockatoos one might otherwise wait a lifetime to see.

TRITON COCKATOO
Cacatua galerita triton

Coming from New Guinea and adjacent islands of the Pacific is the gorgeous triton cockatoo. This cockatoo is still plentiful in New Guinea, and it is occasionally imported into the United States. They are few and costly, averaging, in the late 1970's, about eighteen hundred to two thousand dollars for each pair. Unfortunately, it is frequently confused with its relatives *C. galerita galerita* and *galerita eleonora*.

The triton has feathers in the crest that are broader than in *C. galerita galerita* and divided into three major sections, hence the name of triton. The crest is yellow. The body plumage is white with yellow ear coverts and yellow suffusion under the wings and the tail.

I have seen many tritons in many collections; each one I have witnessed has been most intelligent and quite entertaining. As with many cockatoos, this subspecies seems to be particularly talented in a peculiar but entertaining manner.

Their talent includes dancing up and down, flapping their wings and bobbing their head up and down.

Bill Fetterone of Boston has a pair of triton cockatoos that are both talented. He has named them "Tri" and "Tony." They are easily sexed by eye color. Tri opens her wings wide when Bill says, "Fly like an eagle." Then she extends the triple crest to the greatest extent. Tony, on the other hand, has been taught to walk a tightrope. At the end of his walk he raises his crest and then bows his head as if to curtsy for an audience.

I have seen very few records of *Cacatua galerita triton* breeding in captivity. One such success has been achieved in Illinois by an avid aviculturist who has not one but four pairs of tritons. One of his pairs has gone to nest twice in the last year and a half. Both times two eggs were laid in an old wine barrel which contained only a few shavings. By the time the adults finished with the wine barrel, there were many more shavings. This wine barrel was placed high in an aviary which was six feet high, six feet long and only three feet wide.

The eggs hatched on both occasions and all of the young were successfully raised to fledgling age, at which time they were removed for hand-rearing and handling.

Corn on the cob was the main diet of the adults, although sunflower seeds, carrots and raisins were also eaten. Rice cooked in milk was also presented to the feeding parents. Evidently the babies thrived on this diet when it was regurgitated to them by the parents.

To have such a delightful pair of breeders is very worthwhile and gratifying. I suggested that the owner hold onto this pair. He did not need my persuasion; he still has them.

GOFFIN'S COCKATOO
Cacatua goffini

One of the cutest and smallest of the cockatoo species is *Cacatua goffini*, Goffin's cockatoo. This cockatoo averages about twelve inches in length. I have measured a few of the Goffin's birdskins at various museums; at no time have I seen a bird so uniform as the Goffin's.

Here is a cockatoo that was virtually unheard of prior to

1974 in the United States. I can only recall seeing one pair during the 1960's, and this was outside of the United States.

In the early 1970's, the Japanese lumber industries ravaged the islands of Timor, Kai and Tanimbar, so much in fact that thousands of Goffin's cockatoos were captured and shipped all over the world. Most generally these birds are collected in the jungles of Tanimbar and other islands. They are sold by collectors to a dealer who transports the birds in large numbers to major exporters in Indonesia. From Indonesia these birds are exported to various countries of the world, including the United States. Since literally thousands of Goffin's cockatoos have been imported into the United States, they can be purchased for a comparatively low price. By 1979, one could purchase a Goffin's cockatoo for less than two hundred dollars, thereby making it one of the best buys in the cockatoo world. They are most certainly worth the price as they are docile little cockatoos capable of much comical mimicry. They become extremely tame, making excellent pets.

In color they are generally white with a shading of pink about the feathers of the lores and above and below the eyes. Pink feathers are seen throughout the cheeks and scattered in the throat area. There is a light shading of yellow on the ear coverts. A very pale yellow is noted under the wings and tail. The bill is a light gray. As with most cockatoos, the Goffin's male has a black iris; the female has a reddish brown iris.

There are many pairs of *Cacatua goffini* in many avicultural collections, and there are equally as many single pets in homes and aviaries. John Crella in New York City has three pairs of Goffin's. All are extremely tame and easily handled. His first pair of Goffin's has nested twice within a nine-month period. Each nest contained two eggs. Only one egg hatched each time, with the parents raising the chick to full growth. The second pair has nested once, also laying a clutch of two eggs. Both chicks hatched, but both chicks died at about two or three days of age. The third pair has not yet shown interest in nesting. John has used a large apple tree log for a nesting site for pair number one, another apple tree log is utilized for pair number two and an old pine tree log is ready for number three.

I studied the diet of these Goffin's cockatoos and found that sunflower seeds were the basic staple. Sour milk and whole wheat bread were readily fed and accepted. Hard-boiled eggs mashed with the shell were also fed but not enthusiastically eaten. Several fruits, including apples, pears and bananas, were also offered.

I suggested that safflower seed be introduced to replace 50 to 60 percent of the sunflower seeds. My suggestion to add vitamin E in the form of wheat germ was also put into effect. I had not heard of the feeding of sour milk before this, and I hesitate to state whether this is good or bad. These Goffin's were obviously delighted with the concoction, as they eagerly devoured it.

Those aviculturists owning Goffin's cockatoos must attempt to breed them because there appears to be little future for the Goffin's in the wild. There is literally no future for the Goffin's in the jungles of Timor, Kai and Tanimbar.

RED-VENTED COCKATOO
Cacatua haematuropygia

Also known as the Philippine cockatoo, the red-vented cockatoo is one of the most beautiful of the smaller cockatoos. *Cacatua haematuropygia* is about twelve and one-half to thirteen inches in length. Its plumage is generally white with yellow shading on the ear coverts and yellow shading under the wings. The undertail coverts are red, but the tail feathers are yellow—a most attractive display.

As with Goffin's cockatoo, the red-vented cockatoo has been imported into the United States in large numbers. In 1974, I noted a price list on which was advertised a red-vented cockatoo for $1000. By 1977, they were selling for $150 to $300 each. By 1979, they were up to $350 again.

These attractive cockatoos come from the Philippine Islands. Many of these birds are sold through a whole line of pet shops in Manila. Others are purchased directly from collectors on the various islands who sell the birds to certain dealers for a standard price per bird. In 1977, these dealers were selling red-vented cockatoos for ten dollars to other dealers; by 1979, the price was up to twenty-five dollars per bird.

In early evening, before the cockatoos come home to roost, various collectors throw huge nets over specified trees. Soon the red-vented cockatoos return to roost. At about four in the morning the collectors return to make loud noises with drums and other similar scare tactics. The birds fly into the nets, and many are caught. This is the beginning of a long journey either to Manila or directly to an exporter who ships the cockatoos to the United States.

I have seen many red-vented cockatoos in various pet shops, aviaries and breeding ranches. They can develop into very immaculate, beautiful little cockatoos. They have a small crest which they control so well that one has to look carefully to note that a crest is present. Like other cockatoos, they put up their crest with the least encouragement. Another attractive feature is the strong black eye of the male and the reddish brown eye of the female. I have seen several extremely tame red-vented cockatoos. They love to perch on a person's hand and bob their head up and down in typical cockatoo fashion as if to say, "I'm ready to perform."

Occasionally, however, one of these extremely tame cockatoos will fly away. One such fabulous red-vented cockatoo was always in the habit of perching on her owner's arm. She would do this inside and outside the aviary. One day she simply swooped away, flying to the top of a large pine tree. Our sickened friends tried coaxing her back in every possible way, but they were unsuccessful. During the night hours they attempted to find her, but their efforts were to no avail. The next day they saw her flying in front of their house in the company of a group of blackbirds and grackles. Shortly thereafter she alighted on a treetop. It appeared that the blackbirds were chasing her, or perhaps they wondered what a large white bird was doing in their territory. Our friends again tried coaxing her to no avail. That is the last time they ever saw that cockatoo.

I worry about what happens to runaway birds! Do owls or large hawks seize them? Do they land in someone else's backyard to be retrieved? Certainly, I know that some people pick up a bird of great color on their back porch and find it is a great pet. Many of these people advertise to find the original owners, but others do not.

Another associate had a very tame pair of red-vented cockatoos. He planned to use these for breeding since they were so well feathered and classy. One day he opened their outside flight to walk in and feed them. Much to his shock, the female flew over his shoulder and out into the trees. She evidently kept flying, for he never saw her again.

Red-vented cockatoos have bred in captivity. Harry Loos of Illinois, with whom I have corresponded, once had success with his pair. He used a small garbage can as the nesting site and placed a block of sod upside down on the bottom of the can. The female entered the nesting cavity frequently and she eventually laid two eggs. The male incubated the eggs all day; the female incubated the rest of the night, but she was more restless than the male. Apparently she was not as good a sitter as he. Both chicks hatched and the parents apparently did a good job feeding; however, only one chick grew to maturity. The other chick died at eight days of age.

The red-vented is another cockatoo I would recommend owning. My pair is extremely quiet, although I don't believe we can assess them all by the actions of one pair. Unfortunately, up to this date my pair has never had the urge to breed. I believe it would be advisable to have more than one pair for better breeding results. It seems that if they see what a neighbor is doing, they get interested. Breeding activities in birds seem to increase with same species breeder activity.

LEADBEATER COCKATOO
Cacatua leadbeateri leadbeateri

It is most remarkable to discover rare and unusual birds in the most unusual places. This has occurred to me on at least four occasions in the years 1978 and 1979, and involved one of my favorite cockatoo species, the Leadbeater or Major Mitchell's cockatoo.

While working at the 1979 New Hampshire Cagebird Show, a lady from Australia approached me with a beautiful set of crest feathers (very complete) in a plastic sack. I immediately recognized the crest feathers as that of *Cacatua leadbeateri leadbeateri,* the Leadbeater cockatoo. The lady indicated that she currently lives in Massachusetts, had owned the Leadbeater for several years and was most pleased with the bird. This was the only bird she owned.

Once while presenting a speech on parrots to a group of pheasant and waterfowl enthusiasts, an elderly man approached me to tell me he currently owned a female Leadbeater and had owned her for several years. She, too, was precious to him. He uttered some displeasure that numerous aviculturists, hobbyists and pet shop owners had offered him various amounts of money for the cockatoo, from one hundred to five hundred dollars. Apparently the hopeful purchasers failed to realize that the elderly gentleman knew how high-priced the Leadbeater really was. In the 1970's, thirty-five hundred might have been a better figure.

While attending a dog show in Connecticut, I was approached by a lady with two Maltese dogs. She wished to know if I knew of any male Leadbeaters, since she had owned a majestic female for ten years and wanted to get into breeding. Apparently she secured her bird from an Australian who had lived in her city for a number of years. He wished to sell the bird before his return to Australia. She paid two hundred dollars for the Leadbeater.

Two zoos in New England have pairs of Leadbeater cockatoos: Benson's Animal Farm in Hudson, New Hampshire, and Southwick's Animal Farm in southern Massachusetts. Neither has successfully bred these cockatoos, although Ed Diffendale, the curator of birds for Southwick's, told me that the Leadbeaters were on eggs; but since they are great chewers and since the nest was in a wooden wine cask, it was depressing to Ed when the pair chewed through the bottom of the cask. The eggs fell to the aviary floor and broke.

The pastel beauty of the Leadbeater cockatoo is superb. The crown is white with a strong pastel pink suffusion. The colorful crest of scarlet red is tipped with white, and the extraordinary band of yellow is noteworthy; each crest feather is scarlet at the base with a yellow band in the middle of the feather, then scarlet toward the distal end with a broad tip of white. The face, neck, throat, breast and upper abdomen are dark pastel pink. An even darker rose pink is noted under the wings. The tail and undertail are lighter pastel pink. Primary and secondary flight feathers are deep pink. Since the eye is black in males and reddish brown in females, the species is easy to sex.

Leadbeater cockatoos are rare in the United States because Australia will not allow them to be exported from

Leadbeater cockatoos are beautifully colored birds with crests which have a distinctive color pattern. Photo by Louise Van der Meid.

that country. The cockatoo is found in the central and southwestern parts of Australia.

The Leadbeater or Major Mitchell's cockatoo has been bred successfully in the United States. In New York there is one pair of Leadbeaters which has successfully produced young on three occasions. The owner provides a hollow apple log in a large empty bedroom of his large house. Since the pair of cockatoos has the entire room to themselves (the room is well enforced with chain link to protect the woodwork), they adapted well and accepted the apple log for nesting. They have laid from two to four eggs per clutch, always with 100% hatchability. Incubation was always indefinite; evidently the days were not counted. (Unfortunately, this is one of my big errors also.) Both male and female took turns incubating the eggs. As with other cockatoos, the male incubated the eggs during the day while the female took the chore through the night. Both parents readily fed the babies throughout the fledgling period.

Perhaps one day dedicated aviculturists will be fortunate in securing Leadbeater cockatoos for breeding—if ever the Australian government allows exportation of these cockatoos.

MOLLY'S LEADBEATER COCKATOO
Cacatua leadbeateri mollis

My correspondence with a man from southern Australia was quite rewarding in that he so graciously differentiated the cockatoo he calls Molly's Leadbeater, .*Cacatua leadbeateri mollis,* from the Major Mitchell's or Leadbeater cockatoo, *Cacatua leadbeateri leadbeateri.* John Parker of southern Australia has conveyed to me that large quantities of Molly's Leadbeater cockatoos are seen at various times in the grasslands of southern Australia. His studies indicate that these birds are a rich pastel rose color with a crest of very dark red and white. These birds are not different from Leadbeaters except for the crest; there is no yellow in the forward-curving crest.

John Parker found nesting sites of Molly's Leadbeater cockatoos in hole cavities of various types of trees. On all occasions he found anywhere from one to four eggs; however, the usual clutch was two. His report indicated that it took about eight to nine weeks for the eggs to hatch. Both parents participated in the incubation and rearing of the young.

I have never seen a Molly's Leadbeater cockatoo. To the best of my knowledge, this subspecies is extremely rare in the United States. I did think I saw a pair at the San Diego Zoo recently, but the birds didn't care to show their crests so I was not really sure of their actual identity.

MOLUCCAN COCKATOO
Cacatua moluccensis

One of the more beautiful cockatoos of large stature is the salmon-crested or Moluccan cockatoo. This treasure in pastel pink is coveted by many aviculturists and pet owners. It is found in Indonesia, mainly in the southern Moluccan Islands, but it also is found in Ceram.

I have seen many color variations in various specimens. Some of my Moluccan cockatoos are distinctly white in plumage with only the slightest tinge of pink noted; others have a general plumage color of rich pastel pink throughout. I believe that young birds are almost entirely white and gradually develop the pastel pink as they grow older. Most of my hatchlings have been distinctly white although I can think of two that had rich pinkish shades early in their juvenile plumage. My ten-year-old is very pastel pink.

The Moluccan has a large, broad, backward-curving crest which is deep reddish pink (sometimes salmon-colored) in

Moluccan cockatoos are one of the most appealing cockatoos. Generally they can be easily tamed, they can be taught to do tricks, and they are affectionate and have lively personalities.

color and quite beautiful. The underside of the flight feathers is a lighter pastel pink. However, the underside of the tail feathers shows a remarkable bright yellow in some birds and a lesser yellow in others. In addition, a deep pink color is noted next to the yellow of the underside of the tail. The eye ring is white. Legs and bill are dark gray. When excited, these cockatoos have a habit of raising their crests, stamping their feet and clacking their bills. This unusual behavior is particular to the Moluccan. Another characteristic which is typical of most cockatoos but seen most frequently in the Moluccan is the ability to bring the feathers on each side of the bill up and around to cover most of the bill.

The Moluccan is twenty-three to twenty-four inches in length. My studies of birdskins at Yale University and the

Los Angeles County Museum were worthwhile in that they revealed not only some variation in size, perhaps due to stages of maturity, but also variations in the pastel pink shadings. In a few cases, the pink was almost a deep rose color.

Moluccans have been known as difficult cockatoos to breed in captivity. They apparently do not breed as successfully as umbrella or lesser sulphur-crested cockatoos. They have, however, been bred successfully in the United States in Florida, California, Ohio and New England. On the two occasions when one pair of my Moluccans bred successfully, two eggs were laid. My other pair likewise produced two eggs. Both sexes incubate for the entire incubation period, only getting out of the nest individually for periodic feeding. With one of my breeding pairs, the male left the nest each evening to roost outside. The male and female of the other breeding pair constantly remained in the nesting cavity except when feeding.

Moluccans are exceptional birds for taming. It is rare to find a Moluccan cockatoo that will bite viciously; most of the time this type of parrot will be most affectionate. On more than one occasion my son Daren has tamed a Moluccan cockatoo within one hour. Each time, the individual bird perched on his arm with no apparent fright or even a desire to bite. In fact, Daren could place his fingers between the Moluccan's mandibles with no danger of getting bitten. I have noted that although fully tamed, our Moluccans still stamp their feet and snap their bills when someone approaches their cage or aviary.

One of the more beautiful cockatoos I bred was produced in Ohio. This bird was later sold to Gary and Janet Lilienthal in Massachusetts. They named her "Molly" since the bird's eyes distinguished it as a female—the eyes had a brownish red coloring rather than the distinct black of the male. Gary is able to remove her on his arm from her cage and stroke her head and neck. She apparently loves it.

Our "Cleopatra" and "King Tut" are magnificent birds; they love to eat apples, oranges, grapes and pears, but they particularly love to eat dark rye bread. They prefer eating when no one is looking at them. They also enjoy peanut butter mixed with honey.

The bird that best stood out for its color in the New Hampshire Cagebird Show of 1979 was a most lustrous pastel pink Moluccan cockatoo. Moluccans appear comfortable in an exhibition hall with hundreds of other birds about; in fact Moluccans in general are natural actors and have great appeal.

BLUE-EYED COCKATOO
Cacatua ophthalmica

Here is a cockatoo which is as large as the largest of the greater sulphur-crested cockatoos. Many aviculturists feel that *Cacatua ophthalmica* is much more beautiful than any of the greater or lesser subspecies.

This species is well known for its bright blue eye ring which displays great beauty and contrast to the yellow crest and strong white plumage. There is yellow at the ear coverts as well as yellow shading under the wings and tail. The grayish black beak is moderate in size and certainly not as large as in some of the lesser sulphur-crested subspecies.

This species comes from the islands northeast of New Guinea: New Ireland and New Britain. It is surprising to me that no more than a very few blue-eyed cockatoos are imported into this country each year. They seem to be as rare as *Cacatua galerita galerita*. It is very seldom that one sees a blue-eyed cockatoo advertised by importers or brokers. I do know of a few long-standing pairs and singletons in captivity at the premises of aviculturists and zoos.

One of the most fascinating of all cockatoos I have ever seen was a majestic and extremely docile blue-eyed cockatoo at the Cleveland Zoo in 1970. This character waddled over to us and said, "I'm a cockatoo – I'm a cockatoo." It was an extra-ordinary and unforgettable situation. We immediately fell in love with that cockatoo!

The blue-eyed cockatoo has been bred in captivity. One friend of ours in Arizona has a magnificent pair of blue-eyed cockatoos that are over thirty years or age. They came from a zoo where they had been kept for years. They breed and nest once each year, skipping every third year. The female invariably lays two eggs; they have always hatched, but each time only one baby has survived.

I may, of course, be very wrong, but having knowledge of many fine avicultural collections in New England, I do not know of a single blue-eyed cockatoo in this section of the United States. The blue-eyed cockatoo is an extremely unique bird. I recently viewed one that was part of a bird show, and that blue eyed stole the show! He roller skated, pushed a miniature bicycle, danced in circles and climbed a ladder. Such intelligence gives a cockatoo owner a satisfied feeling that the right avocation has been selected.

The blue-eyed cockatoo is one of the highest priced of the white cockatoos. By late in 1979, only an occasional blue-eyed cockatoo could be found – for twenty-five hundred dollars.

BARE-EYED COCKATOO
Cacatua sanguinea sanguinea

Perhaps the most lovable and amicable of all the cockatoos is the bare-eyed cockatoo or little corella, *Cacatua sanguinea sanguinea*. These are exciting little cockatoos with large irregular naked patches of dark blue about each eyed cockatoos that are over thirty years of age. They came from a zoo where they had been kept for fifteen years. They breed and nest once each year, skipping every third year. The female invariably lays two eggs; they have always hatched, but each time only one baby has survived.

The bare-eyed is a small but nonetheless charming cockatoo. Unfortunately, this bird is not frequently seen in the United States. Photo by Louise Van der Meid.

Cacatua sanguinea sanguinea is found in northern, northwestern, eastern and central Australia. They are still fairly plentiful in the wilds of these sections of Australia. This subspecies is seldom seen imported into the United States, although an occasional zoo or aviculturist has been known to have a single bird or pair of specimens.

Friendly and lovable characteristics are exhibited in their playful mannerisms. I once had a pair of bare-eyed cockatoos that loved to utter sounds of satisfaction while laying their heads in my hands. They each had a habit of almost literally purring like a cat that greatly enjoyed human company. Both birds would take my finger in their beak but would never apply any power to hurt. They loved to be loved and in turn loved to show their interest in a human. I have never seen a bare-eyed cockatoo that was not completely docile and easily handled.

Although my pair never did breed or even attempt to nest through the many years I owned them, there are some bare-eyed cockatoos that have produced young in the United States.

Ed Diffendale, curator of birds at Southwick's Animal Farm in Mendon, Massachusetts, has a beautiful pair of bare-eyed cockatoos that show remarkable intelligence. They too love humans even to the point of coming up with new comical situations to demand attention.

As the years progress into the 1980's, I note that there are fewer and fewer *Cacatua sanguinea sanguinea* in the United States due to the ban on exportations from Australia. There may well be a few more of this subspecies in this country, but you will seldom see very many.

As an exhibition bird, the bare-eyed cockatoo is a true showman. It has such a lively personality that many judges cannot help but look at them more than once, and they indeed take this active personality to be an advantage for the bare-eyed cockatoo. Hopefully they will appear in greater number at bird shows some day soon.

LITTLE BARE-EYED COCKATOO
Cacatua sanguinea normantoni

In comparison to the nominate subspecies, *Cacatua sanguinea sanguinea*, this subspecies is found more often in aviaries in the United States as well as in zoos and as pets in private homes. *Cacatua sanguinea normantoni* is smaller than the nominate subspecies of bare-eyed cockatoo by about two inches. Otherwise, this subspecies has the same gentle, loving type of personality displayed by *Cacatua sanguinea sanguinea*.

This subspecies, which I call the little bare-eyed cockatoo, originates in southern New Guinea, ranging up to the central part of this large island of the south Pacific. It is also found in northern Queensland, Australia.

As previously indicated, it is imported into the United States but not in great numbers. I did see a few in the late 1970's advertised for eight hundred to a thousand dollars each. Some importers appear to have been active in late 1979, but out of this group only about ten tended to occasionally import the little bare-eyed cockatoo.

Like *Cacatua sanguinea sanguinea,* this subspecies is mainly white in color with yellow shading under the wings. Pinkish red feathers are scattered from the lores to the crown as well as through the cheeks and throat area. They also exhibit a large dark blue irregular eye patch which is very characteristic of this species.

Bob Brunelle of Detroit, Michigan, has one little bare-eyed cockatoo that he has had since the 1960's. She has the typical reddish brown eyes of the female cockatoo, unlike the distinctive black eye of the male. Bob tells us that she loves to nestle into his shirt pocket head-first, although she cannot possibly fit completely. She literally gurgles with happiness. She is Bob's favorite over all his other six species of cockatoos.

During a visit to Florida I noticed a very talented and most lovable little bare-eyed cockatoo on exhibition. She seemed to love people; she would place her entire head and neck out of the cage to be stroked and would utter chuckling noises of satisfaction. Although one could spend hour after hour viewing the other birds on exhibit, much of our time revolved around this little cockatoo.

Bill and Irene Bottoms in California have a pair of little bare-eyed cockatoos which they purchased as a pair in 1969 from a zoo. On arrival they placed a large nest box into their newly acquired aviary with the hope that this would induce breeding behavior. It took three years before either of them showed any interest. However, in 1972, both birds frequently entered the nesting site.

During the month of June, 1973, two eggs were laid. Both parents took turns incubating the eggs; the male apparently took the night shift. The female incubated all day and was apparently a good mother. This was unusual because with cockatoos in general, the male will do the daytime incubation. In due time (they didn't get an exact count of the days of incubation) one chick hatched; the other had died within the shell. The parents were allowed to feed, care for and raise the young.

During successive years, this pair has raised successfully one chick each year. They had two clutches in 1977. At no time were two chicks raised, although each time two eggs were produced. On at least two occasions two chicks were hatched, but they were not raised to maturity. This bothers me as I have heard and read that others have had similar problems. Certainly this raising of one chick only per nesting cannot occur naturally in the wild. Apparently in many cases to save the other chick you must raise it by hand-feeding. Bob and Mary are to be congratulated for the success they have reaped.

LESSER SULPHUR-CRESTED COCKATOO
Cacatua sulphurea sulphurea

One of the cockatoos most commonly imported into the United States in the seventies, the lesser sulphur-crested cockatoo, has proved to be extremely popular. *Cacatua sulphurea sulphurea* has a general white plumage as a young bird. As it reaches eight to ten years of age, much yellow diffusion occurs over the entire body. The underside of flight and tail feathers becomes brighter yellow in color, giving a splendid view of "brightness in flight."

This cockatoo is one of the largest of the lesser group; it ranges from eleven to thirteen inches in length. The crest is narrow and bright yellow; it tends to curve forward at the rear. This crest is frequently erected when the bird is approached.

The bill of this subspecies is grayish black in color and

extremely large in comparison to the size of the cockatoo. Actually, the bill of *Cacatua sulphurea sulphurea* seems much larger than that of the greater sulphur-crested cockatoo, *Cacatua galerita galerita*, a much larger bird. This large bill, along with the deep yellow suffusion, is typical of the subspecies *Cacatua sulphurea sulphurea*.

As in most white cockatoos, the iris color of the male is apparently black while in the female one sees a brownish red iris.

I have found that lesser sulphur-crested cockatoos breed readily after the age of five years. I have had little or no luck with younger birds.

My breeding pairs have laid either two or three eggs in their hollow nesting area. Due to the severe wood chewing by this cockatoo, I use galvanized garbage cans as nesting sites. I cut a hole in the side of the can and make sure that the lid is tightly fastened to the top. I insert a perch for proper approach to the hole. Within the can I place black greenhouse soil covered with a few shavings. They seem to enjoy this setup.

After approximately twenty-one to twenty-four days of incubation by both the male and the female, the chicks will hatch. I even had one clutch that took as long as twenty-six days to hatch. I believe the length of incubation time depends on the amount of time both birds actually sit on the eggs, the error of detecting when the incubation really started and the interactions of the male and the female. Occasionally only a single chick was produced; however, upon checking the unhatched egg (or eggs), I found a dead chick in the shell rather than an infertile egg. The eggs are always white in color.

My experiences have proved that it takes the babies about twelve to fourteen weeks to fledge; that is, to leave the nest. I have noted that some babies feather out poorly and slowly; but they appear most beautiful after the first molt.

The lesser sulphur-crested cockatoo can be tamed into a

very friendly and sometimes humorous little bird. Henry Sears of West Virginia has a *Cacatua sulphurea sulphurea* named "Minnie" that loves to dance on her perch. She raises her crest, dances closer and closer to the person watching and then gives the person watching a pecking kiss on the cheek!

I have an older pair of *Cacatua sulphurea sulphurea*. The male, "Pinto," has the most beautiful yellow suffusion I've ever encountered on a lesser sulphur-crested cockatoo. He loves to show his erected crest. When incubation time begins, he sits on the nest all day; the female incubates all night. This is a nice arrangement as some birds of the parrot family have males that could care less about incubating. The female, "Miss Petal," named for the bright yellow ear patches she exhibits (which is also typical of this subspecies), appears to be a very good mother in addition to an excellent hand-tamed pet. She does not become excited when we peek into her nest box. She was hatched in the United States, while Pinto, who has always been more shy, is an import from the Celebes Islands. He arrived at a New York import facility via Indonesia. He had other owners before I was fortunate enough to obtain him. I guess that he is quite old.

Lesser sulphur-crested cockatoos are exhibited quite often. There were no less than seven exhibited at some of the major eastern shows during the 1978 show season. In 1976, a lesser won Supreme Best Bird In Show over all birds at the Annual New Hampshire Cagebird Show.

ABBOTT'S LESSER SULPHUR-CRESTED COCKATOO
Cacatua sulphurea abbotti

The largest of the lesser sulphur-crested cockatoo subspecies is *Cacatua sulphurea abbotti*, which is found only on Solombo Besar Island in the Java Sea.

This cockatoo has pale yellow ear coverts and literally no yellow suffusion on the breast and neck feathers, so it resembles *Cacatua sulphurea occidentalis* except for size—it is larger by two or three inches. The general size of this bird is thirteen to fourteen inches in length. It is one of the sulphur-crested cockatoos that are frequently referred to as the medium sulphur-crested cockatoo. Keep in mind, however, that there are a couple of greater sulphur-crested cockatoos that are also referred to as medium sulphur-crested cockatoos.

Cacatua sulphurea abbotti is frequently imported, but since they are native to only one island I sometimes wonder if the subspecies will disappear. Although it is unconfirmed, I have heard that this subspecies exists in the wilds of the Malaysian jungles; it evidently has been released there from time to time.

I do not have this subspecies in my aviaries; however, I have seen several of these cockatoos in other breeding aviaries and in various homes as pets. They are extremely intelligent and can easily be trained to perform. I do not believe they are good talkers.

Other authors have reported in various articles that the lesser sulphur-crested cockatoo is a very noisy bird. My experiences are quite to the contrary; I find them particularly quiet with only an occasional and not too noisy "CAW." Jerry Hellman, an aviculturist associate, tells me that his eight-year-old pair of *Cacatua sulphurea abbotti* are extremely quiet. They prefer to constantly chew on their perches, and these have to be replaced weekly.

He has been successful in breeding the pair, and each time they go to nest, which is once per year, they produce three fine young. He has been very fortunate to have such a good breeding pair. They are extremely tame and do not get vicious during nesting time. (Certain tame parrots can be excellent breeders, but some become more vicious than wild breeders because they are unafraid of man.)

Cacatua sulphurea abbotti may well be the center of debate among aviculturists and taxonomists for several years. The debate centers around the question: is this really a lesser or is it a medium? Should we have a medium classification just because of a difference in size? My answer to this would be NO.

CITRON-CRESTED COCKATOO
Cacatua sulphurea citrinocristata

One of the most delightful cockatoos in captivity and also one of the more beautiful, due to the colorful orange-yellow crest, is the citron-crested cockatoo. This fairly large cockatoo is fourteen to fifteen inches long and comes from the island of Sumba in the south Pacific. Sumba is one of a chain of islands just south of the Celebes Islands and west of New Guinea.

In addition to having a bright orange-yellow crest, *Cacatua sulphurea citrinocristata* has orange ear coverts. The general plumage is white; there is some yellow diffusion on the underpart of the wings and tail. The crest is superb, and this cockatoo opens it constantly. Each time a member of this subspecies is aroused, the crest is extended and the beautiful orange color is clearly seen. The eye ring is white while the large bill is grayish black. You can sex the males from the females by eye color after approximately six months of age, sometimes before. The female has brownish red eyes; the eyes of the male are black.

The citron-crested cockatoo is extremely popular in the United States. It is imported into this country but not as frequently as other subspecies of the lesser sulphur-crested cockatoo. Pricewise, the citron-crested cockatoo is higher than the other subspecies. When one does see them advertised by various importers and brokers, they average about two hundred dollars more per bird over the lesser sulphur-crested cockatoo.

The citron-crested cockatoo is a popular bird in the United States, but it is not as readily available as some other cockatoos, like the umbrella. A World Wide photo.

Citron-crested cockatoos make excellent pets and tremendous, humorous pranksters. One such citron owned by Paul Jorgenson in Minnesota loves to jump up and down on his perch for a piece of lettuce; he prefers this over all other fruits and vegetables. He constantly raises and lowers his crest as if to give a sign of approval that the lettuce is gratifying. His name is "Sunny," which by the way fits to a certain extent the origin of this subspecies—Sumba Island.

Sunny has learned a few words, probably more than I have heard from any cockatoo. He utters "Hello, Sunny" and "feelings," the latter evidently from the song of the same name. However, there is certainly no tune that accompanies the vocalization. He loves to climb on the shoulder of his owner; he also loves to skip and hop behind his owner on the large green lawn of the house. Certainly, one of the more picturesque scenes I have ever witnessed was this orange-crested cockatoo hopping along on the dark green lawn!

I once had a very tame citron-crested cockatoo. This was a magnificent bird. Although he would never utter a sound, he loved to ride on my arms. I received "Pal" as an adult with no history and kept this beautiful super-tame pet for several years until his death in 1970.

I briefly owned another citron—for one day. I purchased this bird from a well-known aviculturist. The cockatoo seemed almost too tame. I immediately realized that the simple movement of this bird from one home to another created so much stress that I had a very sick bird on my hands. The very next day it died. Upon performing an autopsy I realized there was nothing I could have done for this bird. Aspergillosis, a fungal disease of the respiratory system, was fully evident. This was one of those sad episodes every aviculturist faces periodically. (Coincidentally, the original owner had no intention of replacing the bird or the money, which brings up the fact that the aviculture world in general has much to accomplish on the subject of ethics.)

Citron-cresteds make excellent pets and are fun-loving performers. More captive breeding of these birds must be developed soon. Photo courtesy of Vogelpark Walsrode.

One of the most magnificent young citron-crested cockatoos I have ever met is "Pete," owned by Ed Diffendale, curator of birds at Southwick's Animal Farm in Mendon, Massachusetts. Ed is very successful in the breeding of psittacines and doves. He has successfully bred both scarlet macaws and blue and gold macaws, but his most remarkable accomplishment was twice breeding the citron-crested cockatoo. Pete was his first choice hatch and has developed into a really tame pet. He loves to literally crawl all over Ed and his family, in addition to guests. This young character is unafraid and is most certainly one of the finest specimens of the citron-crested cockatoo around.

Although one generally sees many specimens of the lesser sulphur-crested cockatoo at exhibitions, it is only rarely that we see the citron-crested cockatoo exhibited. I once judged a show where there were sixteen lessers of varying subspecies exhibited, but only one citron was evident. It was in poor feather and so did not do well in the awards.

Hopefully, aviculturists will take hold and attempt to breed more citron-crested cockatoos; then we will be able to see more of these birds at future exhibitions. This is especially important for the citron-crested cockatoo because it is found on only one island, and the wilds there are, like in many other areas of the south Pacific, rapidly being destroyed.

DJAMPEANA LESSER SULPHUR-CRESTED COCKATOO
Cacatua sulphurea djampeana

A splendid subspecies of the lesser sulphur-crested cockatoo occurs in the wild in the Lesser Sunda Islands east of Java in the Pacific. While the nominate subspecies varies from eleven to thirteen inches in length and displays a large bill, this subspecies is generally nine to ten inches in length with a much smaller bill which more appropriately fits the bird. Their general plumage is white; they have yellow ear coverts, while the undersides of the wings and tail are bright yellow. Shadings of yellow occur over the body on adults but not as much as on *Cacatua sulphurea sulphurea*. The much smaller bill is grayish black. Eye color is black in males and reddish brown in females. The periophthalmic ring is white.

These little sulphur-crested cockatoos are extremely cute. When they are approximately four or five years of age, they become very good breeders. They tend to prefer a smaller nest box than the nominate species. I have two pairs of *Cacatua sulphurea djampeana* that are prolific producers of young. They almost always lay three eggs. They are excellent brooders and even better parents. Both of my pairs act in a similar manner when nesting. The male incubates the eggs all day while the female broods on the eggs all night. Apparently little mouth-to-mouth feeding occurs between the parents; however, after the hatchlings arrive, both parents readily feed. I use the smallest garbage can available as a nesting site, with the usual hole and perch in the side. The cover is sealed shut. Each time I have raised *Cacatua sulphurea djampeana*, the incubation period has been twenty-two to twenty-four days.

When the babies do arrive, I have always allowed the parents to feed and care for them — with success each time. I have added much to the diet. Cockatoos, as previously mentioned, are extremely fussy eaters; consequently, I have tried many diets. I have found that breeding cockatoos with babies at their side have readily accepted cooked rice and milk with raisins and shredded carrot. They seem to relish this mixture for the feeding of the young. I also have dishes of sunflower and safflower seeds available, in addition to cut fruits such as apples, pears and bananas. I have tried cheeses and meats (which are devoured by our macaws and Amazons) for higher protein, but generally cockatoos refuse to eat these items. I also place dark whole wheat bread and milk daily in their nesting flights. This is readily eaten.

This subspecies is frequently imported into the United States via Indonesia. The collectors in the jungles of the islands of Pantar and Djampeana, as well as Madu, secure very young cockatoos from their tree-hole nests. The collector gets the equivalent of five dollars for each bird delivered to the island buyer. In turn, the island buyer sells his collection of cockatoos to the Indonesian exporter for ten dollars each. The exporter prepares these birds for shipment to the United States for approximately thirty dollars each. The United States importer will place the new arrivals under thirty-day quarantine, finally selling them for about three hundred dollars each to individual pet shops and for somewhat less to intermediate brokers. In turn the intermediate broker may sell to pet shops or individual breeders or aviculturists. Prices may vary more or less.

Cacatua sulphurea djampeana is a beautiful small cockatoo and has often become a fine tame little pet. The antics of these birds are cute; they love to dance on their perch, showing off by emitting a sharp but not too loud screech.

My two pairs are extremely attractive and very active at all times. In both cases they tend to be somewhat shy when eating. If I come around their flights when they are eating, they fly away from their food. This is simply a trait of the cockatoo; when they eat, they prefer doing it without humans looking on.

OCCIDENTAL LESSER SULPHUR-CRESTED COCKATOO
Cacatua sulphurea occidentalis

A lesser sulphur-crested cockatoo found mainly on Lombok Island next to the famous island of Bali is *Cacatua sulphurea occidentalis*. It differs from *Cacatua sulphurea sulphurea* mainly in color suffusion. It is almost entirely white with pale yellow ear coverts. There is little or no yellow suffusion elsewhere on the bird. *Cacatua sulphurea occidentalis* is frequently imported along with other members of its species. When one sees a mixture of different subspecies they are not difficult to differentiate. This subspecies ranges from eleven to thirteen inches in length.

I do not own any *Cacatua sulphurea occidentalis,* but I know of at least three aviculturists who have breeding pairs. I also know of several individuals who own occidental lesser sulphur-crested cockatoos as pets. As talkers, I would have to rate them fairly low. I have heard some of these cockatoos say "Hello" and an occasional other word, but, in general, this cockatoo and its fellow subspecies are not the better talkers of the parrot family.

The subspecies of lesser sulphur-crested cockatoo are perhaps the most prevalent cockatoos currently seen in the United States. With the possible exception of the red-vented and possibly the Goffin's, they are also the most reasonably priced. Literally thousands of lesser sulphur-crested cockatoos were imported into the United States between the years 1974 and 1979. Many of these were the subspecies *Cacatua sulphurea occidentalis.*

A friend of mine in Detroit owns a pair of this subspecies.

He had such a difficult time getting this pair to eat that he reverted to feeding boiled rice in rice water. To this day, this is all that young pair will eat. I wonder if with such a strict diet this pair will be successful in breeding.

Little is known about the true feeding habits of this cockatoo in the wild, except that fruits, nuts and blossoms are known to be eaten; yet in captivity some cockatoos will not eat the fruits put before them. On the Pacific islands there are, of course, many fruits with which people in this country are not familiar.

LITTLE-BILLED LESSER SULPHUR-CRESTED COCKATOO
Cacatua sulphurea parvula

From the island of Timor, an island where the deforesting activities of lumber companies are widespread, comes the little-billed lesser sulphur-crested cockatoo or Timor cockatoo—*Cacatua sulphurea parvula*.

As the name implies, this lesser has a small bill. Except for this feature, *Cacatua sulphurea parvula* is comparable to *Cacatua sulphurea occidentalis*. (*Cacatua sulphurea djampeana* also exhibits a small bill but has more yellow suffusion, particularly under the wings and tail.) The general body color is white with light yellow ear coverts. There is little or no shading of yellow anywhere else on the body.

The little-billed lesser sulphur-crested cockatoo has been imported only infrequently into the United States. I have seen a few specimens, but all have been individual pets; I have not seen this subspecies in a breeder's collection.

One particular owner of a little-billed lesser sulphur-crested cockatoo is more than pleased with his "Fantasy"—the name for his young female. Fantasy has been taught to climb a miniature ladder and go down the other side. She will run to one end of the table to pick up a small bell, ringing it for an extended period. Interestingly, she doesn't do this for food rewards but rather for someone to scratch her head.

SLENDER-BILLED COCKATOO
Cacatua tenuirostris tenuirostris

The rarest of all white cockatoos is the slender-billed or blood-stained cockatoo, *Cacatua tenuirostris tenuirostris*. This cockatoo is even very rare in its normal habitat, southeastern Australia.

The slender-billed cockatoo, also sometimes referred to as the long-billed corella, is never seen on import listings into the United States due to the strict export ban in Australia. I know of no aviculturists that have breeding pairs of this bird. There are, however, two single specimens, both over twenty years of age, in Delaware and New Hampshire. Both are ideal pets and companions. In both cases the sex is unknown. (Unlike other white cockatoos, this species cannot be sexed by the color of the eyes. Both sexes of the slender-billed cockatoo have dark brown eyes.) There are also specimens of the slender-billed cockatoo at Busch Gardens in Tampa, Florida, and at the San Diego Zoo. Undoubtedly there may be more somewhere in the United States, but I do not know of any others. I am quite sure, however, that only the one specimen is located in New England.

My studies of birdskins at Peabody Museum, Yale University and Los Angeles County Museum reveal that the slender-billed cockatoo is approximately fifteen inches in length. It is characterized by an extremely long bill which is white in color and designed for uprooting bulbs and roots in the wilds of Australia. There is a large grayish blue eye ring. The general plumage is white; however, each birdskin studied had a different array of bright red feathers scattered through the forehead, lores and nape area. These

Rarely seen in the U.S., the slender-billed cockatoo is rare even in its native Australia. Photo by Louise Van der Meid.

red feathers were generally more extensive on the throat and upper breast areas.

I have had little contact with living specimens of the slender-billed cockatoo, although in viewing the bird in New Hampshire, the species appeared as docile and intelligent as the bare-eyed cockatoo. The bird is called "Jennifer," even though the sex is unknown. This bird has become a good pet with no hostility evident, even to strangers.

The slender-bills that I have witnessed at Busch Gardens and San Diego Zoo appeared docile, although it is difficult to distinguish this trait when the bird is perched within a large flight.

It would be difficult to determine the current price of a slender-billed cockatoo—even if one were available. Probably one could purchase a new automobile for a lesser price!

SOUTHWESTERN SLENDER-BILLED COCKATOO
Cacatua tenuirostris pastinator

A dwindling but very important subspecies of cockatoo which may never be seen in the United States (unless a few already exist here) is the southwestern slender-billed cockatoo. It is rare in its normal habitat of southwestern Australia. When it is evident, it prefers those parts of southwestern Australia where the rainfall is heavy.

My study of this subspecies from birdskins revealed a larger bird than *Cacatua tenuirostris tenuirostris* by at least one inch and sometimes two inches. This subspecies, *Cacatua tenuirostris pastinator*, varies from sixteen to seventeen inches in length.

The most notable distinguishing characteristic of this bird is the distribution of the bright red scattered feathers. There are no red feathers on the throat, upper breast or the

Because their exportation from Australia is banned, it is fortunate that rose-breasted cockatoos readily breed in captivity. Photo by Dr. Herbert R. Axelrod.

nape, though you may occasionally find a few tiny red feathers on the lores. Another item which I noted on the birdskins involved the eye ring. Although one would have to study numerous living specimens to confirm this, it appears that the eye ring of this subspecies is a much darker black than that of the nominate race, *Cacatua tenuirostris tenuirostris.* (It must be noted that birdskins do fade and often bill color and eye ring color can be misleading.)

It would be surprising to discover that this subspecies has ever bred successfully in captivity. Little is known concerning their breeding habits, either in the wild or in captivity.

ROSE-BREASTED COCKATOO
Eolophus roseicapillus

Perhaps one of the most fascinating cockatoos native to Australia is the rose-breasted cockatoo or, as it is known by the Australians, the galah. It is most fascinating because it is so darn hard to secure one in the United States. At the end of the 1970's, one could not touch a rose-breasted cockatoo for less than fifteen hundred dollars.

The rose-breasted cockatoo is most attractive and colorful; it is also a devoted and lovable pet. In Australia, however, it is considered a terrible pest. It is indiscriminately slaughtered yet not allowed to be exported to breeders and aviculturists throughout the world.

One good friend of mine spent one year hitchhiking throughout Australia. He reported sightings of numerous dead rose-breasted cockatoos along the roadways; they had evidently been hit by automobiles.

The colorful rose-breasted cockatoo is characterized by a white crown scattered with pink feathers. The crown is a short erectile crest of feathers. A rose-colored eye ring is evident. The face, neck, throat, breast and lower abdomen are deep rosy pink with a few gray feathers showing in the extreme lower abdomen. The under wing coverts are rose.

The Eleonora cockatoo is not the largest of the *galerita* subspecies, but the Eleonora is gaining in popularity in the United States. Photo by Cliff Bickford.

Opposite:
Both the Fitzroy greater sulphur-crested cockatoo (upper photo) and the triton cockatoo (lower photo) breed in captivity, so they might become more readily available in the United States in the future. Photo by Steve Kates.

These baby galahs, or rose-breasted cockatoos, are already beginning to show their rose and gray plumage.

The vent area, tail and secondary and primary wing feathers are gray. The eye of the female is red while the male's eye is black.

Juveniles are distinct for the first few months by having much gray on the breast. Some juveniles have almost all gray breasts, while others have scattered pink feathers.

Jerry Biddle in Indianapolis has been most successful in breeding rose-breasted cockatoos. He has three pairs; all are successful breeders.

In each case, the male manages to put on a marvelous display of courtship. He raises his crest to the utmost and struts with outstretched wings around the female. At the same time he bows his head back and forth, uttering small chuckles of apparent joy. The female flies away hoping the male will chase her. He does! Then they preen each other for hours before copulation finally occurs.

Jerry uses large grandfather clock-type nest boxes which are forty-eight inches high. Almost anything resembling a hollow log with a hole about two-thirds up for entry insures good results. All pairs have consistently produced three eggs each time.

This hybrid cockatoo, the result of a cross between a rose-breasted and a greater sulphur-crested, is unusually attractive. The cheeks and chest are a shade of pastel orange, and the orange-colored crest is intermediate in length between the crests of both parents. Photo by Louise Van der Meid.

These beautiful Leadbeater cockatoos seem to be discussing which of them is going to get to eat a tasty morsel. Photo by Dr. Irvin Huff.

Opposite:
This Moluccan cockatoo is using its foot as a hand—a typical fashion of eating for a cockatoo. Photo by Dr. A.E. Decoteau.

Jerry has been fortunate to have about a 90% hatchability rate. The young are all hand-fed and become very tame. His formula for raising the babies includes only a few drops of milk during the first seventy-two hours of life; the need for nutrition during this first period is satisfied by the internal egg yolk. When the babies are four days old they start getting a mixture of ground sunflower hearts, Pablum, apple sauce and powdered vitamins. Apparently this does a good job since he has had great success raising young to become healthy, well-fledged youngsters with good feathering and coloring.

I have been told by other aviculturists that the rose-breasted cockatoo is readily bred in captivity. There are aviculturists with good breeding pairs having excellent success throughout this nation.

These birds can be most delightful pets. When tamed at a young age, they are extremely docile and very loving. One such rose-breasted cockatoo is owned by Linda Rubin of Brookline, Massachusetts. Linda handles and cares for this cockatoo with tender loving care; in turn, the bird loves to kiss Linda on the lips.

As an exhibition bird, the rose-breasted cockatoo is almost perfect. I seldom see a rose-breasted cockatoo in poor feather. Even rarer is a rose-breasted cockatoo in poor color. All those I have seen at shows and judged myself have been in top condition. I recollect that in 1977 a splendid rose-breasted cockatoo placed high in the south Pacific classes and was judged Best Colored Bird at the New Hampshire Cagebird Show.

Rose-breasted cockatoos are striking and consequently hold the edge on other less colorful birds. If indeed you can secure a pair of rose-breasted cockatoos, do so, since your success in breeding this cockatoo will be practically assured.

Galahs are found through most of Australia. *E.r. roseicapillus* occurs in all but western Australia and has relatively dark colors with a contrasting white crown. The western subspecies, *E.r. assimilis* and *E.r. kuhli,* are paler but have crowns tinged with stronger pink; the eye of *kuhli* is reddish, while that of *assimilis* is grayish.

GANG-GANG COCKATOO
Callocephalon fimbriatum

When one discusses sexually dimorphic characteristics, which means a difference in external characteristics of male and female, one can certainly consider the gang-gang cockatoo, *Callocephalon fimbriatum,* as an outstanding example of a sexually dimorphic bird. Although juveniles resemble the female of the species, the male and female adults are readily discernible by the color of the plumage.

The general plumage of the male is gray. Each feather is edged with a lighter gray color and this gives it a barred appearance. The entire head, upper nape and crest are a bright red color. The feathers of the abdomen and under the tail are edged in a yellow orange. The wings and tail are dark gray.

The female's head and crest are distinctly gray. There appears to be more barring on the female, though each of her feathers is also edged with gray. Breast and abdomen feathers are edged with a pinkish color and occasionally a yellowish green color. If you have the opportunity to see a male and female next to each other, it will be quite evident which bird is the female. The female has a pinker breast than the male, while the male has a brilliant red color on the head.

This cockatoo comes from eastern Australia and northern Tasmania. Like other Australian birds, the gang-gang is banned from export. Consequently it is virtually unknown except for a few specimens that have been in the United States for long periods of time and except for a few birds that were smuggled into this country.

The red-vented cockatoo (left) is one of the smallest and least expensive cockatoos, while the bare-eyed (below), also a small cockatoo, is expensive because it cannot be exported from its native Australia and so is rarely available. Left photo courtesy of Vogelpark Walsrode; lower photo by M. Bonnin.

The blue-eyed cockatoo is one of the larger cockatoos; this one is displaying a cockatoo's ability to "pull" the cheek feathers over the lower mandible. Photo by Cliff Bickford.

I recall seeing a beautiful pair of gang-gang cockatoos which had been smuggled into this country and then seized by officials. Fortunately, they were presented, after a period in quarantine, to a zoo. So rarely does one see a gang-gang cockatoo in this country that when one or more are detected one simply has to stand and study the specimens for an extended period of time.

I noted a splendid pair of gang-gang cockatoos at Busch Gardens in Tampa, Florida, on one of my study visits. They both were about the size of one of the larger subspecies of sulphur-crested cockatoos—about fifteen inches in length. The pair seemed quite intelligent. Apparently quite used to being fed by spectators, they attempted to beg for morsels of food.

Another interesting pair was noted at the San Diego Zoo; this pair was so busy selecting and enjoying flowered seedlings from a eucalyptus branch that I didn't faze them a bit. This was indeed an attractive pair.

I know of no private individuals having gang-gang cockatoos and have seen no records of the successful breeding of these birds in the United States. Only zoos in Australia have shown progress in breeding this classy cockatoo.

YELLOW-TAILED BLACK COCKATOO
Calyptorhynchus funereus funereus

The largest and longest of all cockatoos is the funereal or yellow-tailed black cockatoo. This cockatoo, which is about thirty inches in length, originates in southeastern Australia and Tasmania.

The male is a brilliant black with a brownish sheen throughout. The breast feathers are tipped with yellow and the outside tail feathers carry extensive yellow. The ear coverts are yellow; these are more brilliantly colored in females of the species. The tail of the female has more brown intermingled with the yellow. Both sexes share the same eye color.

The yellow-tailed black cockatoo is extremely rare in the United States. I have seen one specimen at the San Diego Zoo; it was housed with a white-tailed black cockatoo. In Busch Gardens in Tampa, Florida, I noted a pair some years ago. I don't know whether or not they are still alive. Although the possibility exists, I know of no aviculturists who own specimens of the yellow-tailed black cockatoo. To the best of my knowledge, this species has not been bred in the United States.

It is amazing to me to note the complete contrast in popularity between white and black cockatoos. Apparently white cockatoos have a much greater demand among pet owners, aviculturists and zoological gardens. Blacks of all species are much rarer in captivity, even though in Australia there is at least one white, the slender-billed cockatoo, that is closer to extinction. One reason could be the extreme wariness of the black cockatoos. Another involves the availability of nests. Apparently, nesting areas of the black cockatoos are more difficult to locate and to get to when located. When found they inevitably contain only one chick. Hopefully, nest "robbers" will begin to think twice before taking a single chick away.

WHITE-TAILED BLACK COCKATOO
Calyptorhynchus funereus baudinii

Similar to the yellow-tailed black cockatoo is the white-tailed black cockatoo of southwestern Australia. The male and female appear morphologically similar to the yellow-tailed black cockatoo except for the light color. Ear coverts and tail color are distinctly white in both sexes, although the female is readily distinguished from the male.

I have seen even fewer white-tailed black cockatoos in this country than yellow-tailed black cockatoos. There is

The bright yellow forward-curving crest and yellow cheek patch of the lesser sulphur-crested cockatoo can be clearly seen in this side view head-study. Photo by Cliff Bickford.

Opposite:
The citron-crested cockatoo has a rich orange-yellow crest and dark yellow ear coverts. Photo by Cliff Bickford.

one beautiful specimen at the San Diego Zoo. A pair belongs to an avid aviculturist who lives in Iowa and with whom I have been acquainted for many years. (He wishes anonymity because his birds are so very rare.) His pair of white-tailed black cockatoos is extremely docile and readily handled. Neither has shown any indication of breeding in the eighteen years he has owned them, although a nest log is always present.

GLOSSY COCKATOO
Calyptorhynchus lathami

The rarest of the cockatoos in the United States, although not thought to be the rarest in Australia, is the glossy or glossy black cockatoo, *Calyptorhynchus lathami*. Many Australians have indicated to me that the slender-billed cockatoo is much rarer than the glossy cockatoo.

The male and the female are easily distinguished. The male has a brownish head, nape, back and breast, and the wings and tail are black. In the central areas of the lateral tail feathers, a bright red region is distinguishable. The vent area is also red.

The female tends to be shorter by two inches, has a lighter brown head and crest and exhibits yellow on the cheeks, lores and scattered sparsely through the nape. The wings and tail are black, and the middles of the lateral tail feathers have much red intermingled with black.

Eye color is similar for both sexes; this is something which is generally common to all black cockatoos, as well as one white cockatoo, the slender-billed.

Several years ago I did see a pair of fantastic glossy cockatoos in a private zoo in Puerto Rico. They were exhibited in a large planted aviary, but the plants were completely denuded by the cockatoos. A large square nest box was evident in the corner of the aviary. It contained a large opening. The owner indicated to me that he had successfully bred the pair on three occasions, but I could not find out what had happened to any of the offspring. He stated that the female had laid only one egg on each occasion, nesting two years apart each time. Only the female incubated the egg—for a period of about thirty days. When hatched it was cared for by only the female. It was interesting to note that the male had interest in copulating and displaying but nothing else. It is also noteworthy that a single egg was laid each time. Most cockatoos lay two eggs.

RED-TAILED BLACK COCKATOO
Calyptorhynchus magnificus

Extremely rare in the United States but quite prevalent in northern Australia is the large, magnificent red-tailed black cockatoo, *Calyptorhynchus magnificus*. This bird is also sometimes referred to as the Banksian cockatoo. In the wild it is known to feed on seeds from eucalyptus, acacia and other trees.

This species is so rare in the United States that very few aviculturists and zoos have breeding pairs. I recall seeing one outstanding pair at Busch Gardens in Tampa, Florida. The male was very docile and simply loved to come to the cage end and talk to park visitors as well as display his fine feathers to them. He loved to take peanuts and popcorn from passersby. He appeared to be about twenty-seven inches long, which is typical of males. The female appeared an inch or two smaller. The female did not attempt to come to the edge of the cage to beg for attention and food as the male did.

Another pair, more sophisticated, is housed at the San Diego Zoo. Both male and female are attractive, even though they are dimorphic in that the male and female are colored differently. The male is black in general color with some grayish brown in some of the feathers. The central tail feathers are black, and the outer feathers of the tail are

The rose-breasted cockatoo or galah of Australia exhibits a lovely contrast between the deep rose on the breast and the light charcoal-gray on the wings. Photo by Cliff Bickford.

Opposite:
The slender-billed cockatoo is rarely seen in the United States, and it is also rare in its native Australia. The long beak is used for rooting for food. Photo courtesy of San Diego Zoo.

There are, unfortunately, no known reports of red-tailed black cockatoos being successfully bred in the U.S., though they have been bred in captivity in their native land. Photo by M. Davis.

black with a bright red broad band. The bill and legs are dark gray. The female is a dark grayish black and brown with each feather bordered with yellow; this gives a somewhat overall mottled effect. It appears that there are numerous yellow spots on the head and neck as well as on the crest. Feathers under the wings are more yellowish and orange. The tail band which is the counterpart to the male's is orange-yellow.

It should be noted that eye color cannot help to distinguish the sexes, but it is not needed in this species anyway.

To the best of my knowledge, this species of cockatoo has not been bred in the United States. It has, however, been bred in captivity in New Zealand as well as in Australia.

One very good aviculturist in Florida, who prefers to remain anonymous, has four red-tailed black cockatoo specimens—three females and one male. To date there has not been any attempt at breeding. Indeed, he has seen no fighting or signs of jealousy among the three females. He has certainly attempted to induce them to breed by placing a large nesting log within the aviary and by increasing their vitamin intake and increasing the total protein consumption. His birds are all hand-tame.

The red-tailed black cockatoo is found in all parts of Australia moist enough to support it but is uncommon or rare. There are four barely distinguishable subspecies.

BLACK PALM COCKATOO
Probosciger aterrimus

I would venture to state that the black palm cockatoo is today the most costly of all parrots. Small numbers of them are available—if you can afford five thousand dollars a bird!

I well recall the first black palm I ever saw. The typical charcoal color was a great contrast to the bright red cheek patches. I had always thought the palm to be a solid black color. Rather, the general plumage is a charcoal gray. The cheek patches, which are bare skin, vary in color from pale pink to crimson red. An excited palm will exhibit a bright red cheek patch while a docile palm will show a dull pink patch. The thighs are bare and gray. The bill is grayish black, and the upper mandible of the male is much larger than that of the female. The majority of specimens originate in New Guinea as well as in the surrounding

A rose-breasted cockatoo costs about two dollars in Australia but over $1500 in the United States. Photo by Cliff Bickford.

Opposite:
The yellow-tailed black cockatoo (upper left photo), the female red-tailed black cockatoo (upper right photo) and the white-tailed black cockatoo (lower photo), like all black cockatoos, are extremely rare in the United States. Upper left photo by Steve Kates; upper right photo and lower photo by L. Robinson.

150

A black palm cockatoo is probably the most expensive cockatoo available today. This bird is truly regal—dark gray in color with a cheek patch which changes color depending upon the bird's state of excitement. Photo by James M. Gorman.

islands, such as Aru, some Papuan islands and Cape York in northern Australia.

It amazes me to discover individual palm cockatoos in private collections in the oddest of places. A couple of good friends who exhibit dogs of various breeds also have a grand collection of parrots. Included in their collection is a fabulous palm cockatoo. The palm is extremely steady on his perch and can be handled by the owners; however, no one else, including my wife and me, could approach the aviary.

In contrast, another very good friend of ours in Portland, Maine, has a palm that is very docile; he can be handled by anyone. He can repeat his name, "Peter," quite distinctly. Peter loves to take a bath; only he gives anyone nearby a bath as well. His diet consists of coconut which is given fresh daily as well as Brazil nuts, apples and pears. He easily cracks the Brazil nuts with his strong beak.

Another aviculturist in Springfield, Massachusetts, has within his aviary one of the most extensive collections of psittacines in New England. Among this collection is a large grayish black palm cockatoo. His name is "Paleface." His owner has explained the reason for the name. Paleface gets irritated frequently; consequently the red skin patch becomes increasingly bright and then becomes pale upon relaxation. With such a constant surge of bright red to very pale on his face, his name just seemed to be "made" for the bird.

This palm cockatoo loves to dance on his perch; he moves from one end of the perch to the other, moving up and down vertically during the entire escapade. His favorite food is papaya when he can get it. He also loves fresh coconut and the usual sunflower seeds.

The palm cockatoo is well represented at Busch Gardens in Florida, where it is exhibited in a beautiful and enormous aviary with nesting facilities and plenty of perching facilities. The San Diego Zoo exhibits at least one pair of palms, and the palm is well represented at the Los Angeles Zoo also. At least two of the zoos in Puerto Rico have had specimens of this splendid cockatoo.

Records of breeding the palm cockatoo are sparse. One aviculturist in Illinois has informed me that his pair did nest in a huge hollow apple tree log. The female laid one large egg the size of a bantam chicken egg. The pair incubated the egg intermittently, but the egg never hatched.

The three subspecies of *Probosciger aterrimus* differ in only minor details and are found through most of New Guinea, a few adjacent islands and extreme northern Queensland, Australia.

The immense capability of the huge beak of a black palm is shown in this close-up of the head. Photo by Cliff Bickford.

INDEX